John Cairns

The Jews in Relation to the Church and the World

A Course of Lectures

John Cairns

The Jews in Relation to the Church and the World
A Course of Lectures

ISBN/EAN: 9783744708432

Printed in Europe, USA, Canada, Australia, Japan

Cover: Foto ©Lupo / pixelio.de

More available books at **www.hansebooks.com**

THE JEWS IN RELATION TO THE CHURCH AND THE WORLD.

THE JEWS IN RELATION TO THE CHURCH AND THE WORLD.

A Course of Lectures
BY
REV. PROFESSOR CAIRNS, D.D.   REV. CANON COOK, M.A.
REV. PROFESSOR LEATHES, M.A.
RT. REV. BISHOP CLAUGHTON, D.D.   REV. DONALD FRASER, D.D.
REV. PROFESSOR BIRKS, M.A.

WITH A PREFACE BY THE
RIGHT REV. BISHOP PIERS CLAUGHTON, D.D.,
Canon of St. Paul's, Chaplain-General of the Forces, etc., etc.

London:
HODDER AND STOUGHTON,
27, PATERNOSTER ROW.
MDCCCLXXVII.

Hazell, Watson, and Viney, Printers, London and Aylesbury.

PREFACE.

THE accompanying Lectures were delivered at the request of a Committee which was itself the result of a meeting of Clergy and Laity held at the Cannon Street Hotel, and of a very interesting discussion which then took place on the subject of the Jews. The Conference was not in itself of a missionary character, nor are its lectures to be viewed as missionary addresses: they were undertaken by the Lecturers at the desire of the Committee, in some instances at considerable inconvenience to themselves; and the views which they express are those of men who have not come prominently forward as having special opinions on the very interesting subject of which they treat, but who, in the midst of much thought and study on kindred subjects, have naturally formed a judgment upon this, which lies at the root of our religious belief. The Lectures were composed without previous consultation amongst the authors, and it is not to be wondered at (nor scarcely to be regretted) if, in some instances, they travel over the same ground, and touch the same points with similar or with varying opinions. This, indeed, renders their general agreement the more valuable, whilst it must give somewhat greater weight to the several judgments of those who express them. It is fair to add that to a certain extent the writers themselves are taken at a disadvantage, as they may appear to be giving judgment on very momentous questions without special preparation. For what they lose by exposing themselves to this charge they will, there is good reason to believe, find ample compensation in the evident candour and courage they have shown for good, risking cheerfully some loss of repute for deep study, when invited to discuss, almost without notice, the tenets of a very ancient and remarkable race, and to treat of the very oldest form of religion—that religion, be it remembered, itself the actual evidence of their own, its Revelation in part the authority on which it depends, and its history the fountain from which it springs.

The Lectures address themselves to three classes of hearers—each class, it is believed, represented amongst those who listened to them apparently with increasing attention during their delivery. They appeal incidentally to Christians, not as those for whom they were specially intended, but as the body, as it were, which they represented, in urging (though indirectly) the claims of the later Revelation upon those who were the recipients of the first. Christians could not but be interested in an attempt to draw the attention of the Jewish race to their actual position, as holding a creed so closely affecting their own. Nor do we deny that *virtually* these Lectures must be taken as an appeal to the generous candour of Jews to look upon Christianity at least with less hostile feeling, as being the *fulfilment*, not the contradiction, of their own rich promises and Divine Law. It is unnecessary to say more on the character which these Lectures must present to the Christian portion of the audience.

There is another section of that audience which may be assumed to have listened to remarks on Judaism and Christianity with interest, though not perhaps with favour,—those who dislike anything which assumes the existence of a Revelation, and who would especially distrust Judaism, as containing the evidence of its own verity and that of the Christian religion besides. To these I would point out the significance of the words they heard, (or may yet read,) as the utterances of men worthy, surely, of their attention, on a subject which they may have failed sufficiently to consider in their category of evidence, and to point out the absolute agreement of the Jewish and Christian Scriptures as bearing testimony to certain facts. To say this is not to impute to them a carelessness not shared by others. Too many Christians, it is to be feared, look upon Jews simply as they would on Mahommedans, or with more disfavour, from the memory of one terribly dark page in their history. To the Freethinker, or to the careless Christian, these Lectures present a very important and profitable study: to either, the perusal of them can scarcely fail to be of service, and (surely we may add) of deep interest.

To Jews, and especially in proportion to their education and higher intellectual advancement, these Lectures are presented—with the deepest respect, and an earnest hope that they may be accepted —as they are intended—as the simple honest treatment of a most important question, "Is the present condition of this remarkable race that which from their own Scriptures they must—as all other thinking men—conclude it was designed that it should be? It is to be regretted that, in some quarters, another (and a less worthy) estimate appears to have been made of the spirit in which this movement has been made—the mere expression of difference has been taken to be an attack upon them as a people. Such views will not prevail with the intelligent and the well-informed amongst the representatives of the race dwelling amongst ourselves ; and to these the Lectures are addressed by those who, they may be assured, whether the Lecturers themselves are considered, or the Committee who invited them, have no feelings towards them but those of sincere respect, deep interest, and a sure belief in the great and glorious destiny for which in the mysterious counsels of God they are designed.

CONTENTS.

	PAGE
I. THE GREATEST HISTORICAL MARVEL, AND HOW TO ACCOUNT FOR IT	1
BY THE REV. PROFESSOR CAIRNS, D.D.	
II. CHRISTIANITY THE JUSTIFICATION OF THE MOSAIC ECONOMY	31
BY THE REV. CANON COOK, M.A.	
III. THE RELATION OF THE JEWS TO THEIR OWN SCRIPTURES	61
BY THE REV. PROFESSOR STANLEY LEATHES, M.A.	
IV. THE RELATION OF THE JEWS TO THE NATIONS AT LARGE	89
BY THE RIGHT REV. BISHOP CLAUGHTON, D.D.	

		PAGE
V.	THE COMPARATIVE EFFECTS OF JUDAISM AND CHRISTIANITY UPON THE WORLD	107
	BY THE REV. DONALD FRASER, D.D.	
VI.	THE TRUE PREROGATIVE AND GLORY OF THE JEWS	135
	BY THE REV. PROFESSOR BIRKS, M.A.	

I.
The Greatest Historical Marvel: How to Account for it?

BY

REV. PROFESSOR CAIRNS, D.D.

I.

THE GREATEST HISTORICAL MARVEL: HOW TO ACCOUNT FOR IT?

TO myself and other lecturers in this series the subject is so interesting, that we may well bring to it any powers of argument that we may possess, and also so new, that we may well be excused by Jewish hearers if we fail in anything to catch their point of view, or if we assume through imperfect information any thing which they deny. For myself, I have no wish but to conduct this discussion with perfect fairness; and my only regret is, that, having been engrossed till quite recently with work that could not be intermitted, I have had less time than I should otherwise have taken to consult authorities on the Jewish side. I have, however, for a considerable number of years studied the Jewish controversy. I have carefully read, to the best of my ability, the Old Testament in the original, and such Jewish interpretations of it as are reported in the standard Christian commentators, especially in regard to the Messiah. I have gone over the objections to Christianity put by Celsus into the mouth of his Jew, as met and replied to by Origen. I have studied fully the dialogue of Justin Martyr with the Jew Trypho, and also the long and interesting debates maintained by Eusebius in his "Gospel Preparation" and "Demonstration;" and of more modern literature, omitting much that is less formal, I have travelled through the friendly conference (*Amica Collatio*) between the learned Jew Orobio, and the Christian theologian, Limborch, towards the end of the seventeenth century, in which the argument on both sides is pretty well exhausted. In travel, also, and residence on the continent, as well as at home, I have had no small discussion with non-Christian Jews, and with Jews who had become Christians, and have learned something of the internal conflicts in the Jewish communion, and of the reactions of modern opinion upon the Synagogue as upon the Christian Church from the days of Spinoza to our own. In ordinary circumstances, to mention these or similar particulars would savour of egotism or of impertinence. But the Jew is entitled, when addressed in an argument, to know something beforehand of his fellow-reasoner—at least to the extent of such an interest being proved in his national literature and distinctive religious opinion as shall be some guarantee for sympathy of spirit, earnestness of aim, and general accuracy of representation.

It falls to me, therefore, in the plan of these Lectures, to consider Christianity, including Christ Himself, as a sign and a wonder in history, upon any theory of explanation whatsoever, and specially to examine the theory to which a Jew is shut up so long as he disowns Christianity, and regards it either as delusion or imposture. The difficulty exists, not for Jews only, but for Gentile unbelievers, according to their different schools of more reverent, or more defiant negation; but I shall endeavour to look at the matter more from a Jewish point of view; and, as for this I must separate the Jew from the unbeliever, I shall generally assume the literal truth of the Old Testament as a miraculous history, and as the history of a revelation, though here and there also meeting the unbelief which has entered into Jewish circles, and which, to find Him whom we call Christ, would need likewise to recover Moses and the Prophets.

I shall, in conducting this argument, then, ask three questions. *First*—How came Christianity as a distinctive doctrinal and moral system? *Secondly*—How came the historical character and picture of Jesus Christ? and *Thirdly*—How came the historical success, prevalence and influence of Christianity, with its prospects and tendencies as contrasted with the present state of Judaism?

I. *First*—How came Christianity as a distinctive doctrinal and moral system? While the Christian contends that his religion is not distinctive, at least radically, so far as the Old Testament itself is concerned, he must hold, and the Jew must agree with him, that it is distinctive as contrasted with the modern Jewish interpretation. The rationalist, indeed, may bring his Christianity very near to modern Judaism, and even to Mahometanism; but the ordinary Christian must contend for the world-wide difference between modern Judaism and Christianity; and the Jew must accept this assertion, if Christianity, as taught by Christ and His apostles, involved such doctrines as the Trinity, the Incarnation, the atonement of Christ as the Son of God for human sin, the justification of the soul by His blood, the sanctification of men by the Spirit of God as His agent, and the coming of this God-Man from the heaven where He reigns to raise the dead and judge the world. If these things ever existed, as the Christian believes, in the *rôle* of the Old Testament Messiah, they have each and all been dropped in the recent beliefs of Judaism, and Christianity stands out against it, contrasted in these great distinctive articles which are its very foundation and substance. How then did this great system of Christian doctrines originate? It is very inconvenient for the Jew that he cannot accept the hypothesis of the unbeliever, that these doctrines were Jewish errors taught in the Old Testament and participated in by Jesus and His apostles, who, having their minds filled with Old Testament prophecies and representations, transferred all to the supposed Messiah, Jesus of Nazareth, as an actual person. This theory of Strauss will not suit the orthodox Jew, for he cannot afford to have the Old Testament made the matrix out of whose shadowy outlines the doctrines of the Trinity or of the Deity of the Messiah may have arisen; and out of whose more distinct teachings and emblems, in regard to sacrifice, the rest of Christianity may have been developed.

The Jew is bound to repel every plausible derivation that carries up the Christian doctrine of the Trinity, for example, to the creation-narrative: "Let *us* make man in our image, after our likeness," etc.; that sees, in Proverbs viii. 30, a son brought up with an eternal Father; and that finds in Daniel's vision of the Son of Man coming with the clouds of heaven, the source of the impression of Jesus and His followers, that such an appearance was to precede and usher in a supernatural kingdom. And likewise the Jew is bound to protest with all vehemence against the Epistle to the Hebrews as a right interpretation of Leviticus and of the Mosaic ordinances of sacrifice, since the Jew has now excluded the idea of expiation from the work of the Messiah, and stands at the greatest possible remove from the words of Jesus in Matt. xx. 28, "The Son of Man came not to be ministered unto, but to minister, and to give his life a ransom for many." There is indeed in the Jewish prayer-book a frequent and earnest confession of sin, more especially on the day of annual Atonement, of which this is a specimen: "O my God, before that I was formed I was incapable; and now that I exist, am as though I had not been formed: dust I am while I live, how much more so at my death: behold, I am in thy presence as a vessel full of shame and dishonour. Let it be willed before thee, O Lord my God, and the God of my fathers, to enable me that I sin no more, and let the sins which I have sinned before thee be erased through thine abundant mercies; yet not by means of chastisements and sore sicknesses" (p. 136, *Tephilloth*, London, Alexander, A. M., 5548). And there are also repeated prayers for the coming of the Messiah, of which this, one of the series of petitions on the same anniversary day, is an example: "And herewith, O Lord, grant glory to thy people, praise to them that fear Thee, and hopes to those that seek Thee, and confidence unto those that wait upon Thee; joy to Thy land and gladness to Thy city; and a flourishing restoration of the kingdom of David Thy servant, and a splended light to the son of Jesse, Thine anointed, speedily in our days" (*Tephilloth*, p. 119). But it is to be noticed that, nowhere in the Jewish prayer-book, are any of the functions of what Christians call a Mediator between God and man ascribed to the Jewish Messiah. He has no special place in connexion with the pardon of sin; and in another of these anniversary prayers he is put on the same level with the petitioners and their fathers: " Our God and the God of our fathers shall cause our prayers to ascend, and come, approach, be seen, accepted, heard, and be thought on, and be remembered in remembrance of us, and in remembrance of our fathers, in remembrance of Thy anointed Messiah, the Son of David Thy servant, and in remembrance of Jerusalem, Thy holy city, and in commemoration of all Thy people, the house of Israel before Thee, to a good issue, with favour, with grace, with compassion, and with a happy and peaceable life, on this day of Atonement " (*Tephilloth*, p. 130). It is true that it forms an article in the Jewish creed (the 12th of 13) that a Messiah shall come. But this is expressed in the vaguest terms: " I believe with perfect faith in the coming of the Messiah, and though notwithstanding he tarrieth, I will await in expectation of his daily coming " (*Tephilloth*, p. 2); and of the prayers which shed light upon his expected work, none is perhaps more definite than the following: " O the merciful, He shall make us worthy to behold the days of the Messiah, and that we may enjoy life in futurity " (*Tephilloth*, p. 142); and this longer prayer for the three festivals, which (though the Messiah is not mentioned in it), evidently sums up his work, as being what He is called elsewhere, a גאל or Redeemer: " For reason of our sins we were driven from our land, and removed far distant from our territories, that we are unable to go up for to appear and to worship, and to perform our duty before Thee in the temple of Thy choice, the great and sanctified temple where we called unto Thy name, for the sake of the power which was sent against Thy sanctuary. Let it be willed before Thee, O Lord our God, and the God of our fathers, most merciful King, again to have compassion upon us and upon Thy sanctuary, and through Thine abundant mercies quickly rebuild it and magnify the glory thereof. O, our Father, our King, manifest the glory of Thy kingdom over us speedily, shine forth and be exalted over us in the sight of all living; and gather our dispersions from among the nations; erect Thou an ensign and assemble us that are scattered from the extreme parts of the earth, and conduct us, O Lord, our God, unto Zion, Thy city, with rejoicing, and unto Jerusalem, the city of Thy sanctuary, with everlasting joy, that we may there perform before Thee the offerings of our duty, the continual offering according to their order, and the additional offering according to their institution. And the additional offering of this Sabbath-day, [or] of this day of the feast of unleavened bread, [or] of this day of the feast of weeks, [or] of this day of the feast of tabernacle, on this eighth day of the feast of solemn assembly, will we observe and offer unto Thee with love" (*Tephilloth*, pp. 114, 115).

We thus see how limited is the function of the

Jewish Messiah according to the prayer-book. He has nothing to do with priesthood or sacrifice, save only restoring the Old Testament ritual in Jerusalem according to the law of Moses. He has no influence in the pardon of sin, and may, for anything that appears, be himself a sinner. He is not in any proper sense a prophet, much less a lawgiver like Moses, for the prayer-book carefully exalts Moses and guards his law as in all things unchangeable; and it is even doubtful whether Orobio has, in the prayer-book, anything that supports his view that the Messiah is to make the true religion universal; for though this seems to follow from other statements, such a result is nowhere directly connected with the Messiah's name. He is a mere king or ruler, who, like Joshua, conquers a territorial centre for the chosen people, and thence develops and extends the spirit of their unchanged Mosaic institutions; but he is not clothed with any transcendent greatness, intellectual or spiritual, and is the simple servant of Jehovah, bringing round a change necessary to the corporate well-being of the Jewish people, but in no way needful to their individual salvation, which solely depends on their adherence to Moses, and on God accepting their very partial conformity to the original law, and covering the rest. We are thus in a position to see how stupendous a revolution, tried by Jewish ideas, in religious thought, was brought in by Christianity, and how far modern Judaism is from being able to explain its origin. Christianity, indeed, borrowed a portion of its doctrine, from Judaism as still held, the unity and perfections of God, the moral law, and the prospect of immortality both for soul and body. But in regard to all characteristic points, Christian belief was in flagrant contrast. The Jew, according to the prayer-book, while confessing sin and deprecating punishment, had so slight an idea of its evil, that he never dreamed of God finding any difficulty in pardoning it; the Christian, though believing it pardonable, regarding it as so deadly, that a whole mighty system of mediation had to be introduced, rising up to a Trinity in the Godhead, an Incarnation of the Son of God, and a voluntary sacrifice of this Great Being for the expiation of human guilt. The Jew in his prayer-book can speak, indeed, of atonement, but it is of atonement made by himself, as when he prays, " Alas, through our iniquities Thy holy temple was destroyed, and there is not unto us temple nor priest to expiate for us; therefore let it be willed from Thy presence, that the diminishing of my fat and blood which I have consumed this day may be as the fat that was laid on the altar before Thee, and be accepted from me" (*Tephilloth*, p. 40). And again, " If the time is approached that I am to die, O let my death be an expiation for all my sins, iniquities, and transgressions, wherein I have sinned, offended, and transgressed against Thee, from the day of my existence on the earth until this day" (*Tephilloth*, p. 162). But the Christian utterly shrinks from any atonement made by himself or any other sinful creature, and looks to the Incarnate Saviour as the Lamb of God that taketh away the sin of the world.

How, then, were these doctrines introduced into human thought and literature—doctrines which, though the Christian regards them as a development, and the greatest development of Judaism, the Jew utterly denies to have any trace of themselves or any justification in the Old Testament? They originated, as an absolute creation, according to the Jew, in the teaching of Jesus of Nazareth and His immediate disciples. There is no room for any theory that they were gradually formed in the Christian Church. They appear in the debate of Justin with Trypho, as they would do in a modern discussion, and they are found, not only in the earliest Gospels, but in the four Epistles of Paul to the Corinthians, Galatians, and Romans, before the year 60 of the Christian era, as the most extreme rationalism acknowledges. They came, then, into birth at once, if we are to follow the Gospels, mature in the mind of Jesus; or, if we try to construct a theory by setting the Gospels aside, they were devised by His followers as a means of obviating the shame of His death, or were hinted at by Himself, when He anticipated its occurrence. Is this credible upon Jewish premises? The thoughts involved are confessedly great, startling, and gigantic, and they are also parts of a coherent system, which, starting from the infinite evil of sin, brings in a Divine yet voluntary sacrifice, and connects the work of expiation with that of regeneration and sanctification, through another manifestation of the one Godhead. The very connexion claimed by this system with the Old Testament as a fulfilment of the great hope of a Messiah and kingdom of God, and as the antitype of the wonderful and significant ritual of sacrifice, indicates a farther reach and vastness of thought, which the candid Jew, in disowning it, must respect; but looking simply at the naked greatness and loftiness of the ideas in themselves, is it at all reasonable to say that they were the dreams of a solitary and uneducated Galilean, or the hallucinations of a Rabbi like Saul, who left the synagogue, and gave for his otherwise inexplicable defection this justification, that the crucified Nazarene was an incarnation of the Divinity, and an atoning Messiah hitherto undreamt of in the schools of Rabbinism? Could the radical principles of Christianity have originated thus by a sudden descent from the clouds or emergence from the abyss, more especially when we find the Old Testament idea of the perfections of God and the supreme duty of loving Him so faithfully adhered to; when we find a morality preached, which Orobio confesses is so pure, that anyone practising it would live like an angel (*Amica Collatio*, p. 78), and when, not least, Christ and His apostles, in disregard of the allegation that the Old Testament doctrine of immortality was obscure or uncertain, unhesitatingly strike into the line of their Pharisaic opponents, and defend it against the Sadducees? Are these indications of tender sensibility of conscience, of sound thought, and of wise discrimination, compatible with the Jewish hypothesis that such men were abandoned by God to a wild and monstrous hypothesis respecting His own Being, and His mode of forgiving and renewing sinners; or that they actually fabricated, on the spur of the moment, and *ex post facto*, (as nothing of the kind is seen in the faith of the disciples up to their Master's death,) this sweeping series of dogmas, alike in defiance of reason and Old Testament Scripture, to retrieve the shame of the crucifixion, and to turn that into a Divine sacrifice which was a merited, or at least not unnatural, punishment for blasphemy or incendiary delusion? That Christ and His apostles were deceivers, happily the Jews in general no longer hold; but it is put to the calm consideration of all, whether they could, under the conditions which alone the Jewish belief allows, have either intellectually or morally originated so vast and stupendous a scheme, and whether it is not still to the Jew an unexplained marvel, and one that should lead him farther for its solution?

II. The *second* question connected with this enquiry is, How came the historical character and picture of Jesus Christ? This is so far included in the discussion of Christ's doctrine, but not mainly; since it is one thing to be the author of an epoch-making doctrine, and another thing to be the exhibitor and standard in one's own person of a perfect moral life. Now this honour the Christian claims for Jesus Christ, and he presses the claim on the attention of the Jew. This controversy in regard to the life of Jesus has lately agitated the public mind in all intellectual communities, and though non-Christian Jews have not contributed much to it, they doubtless have not been insensible to its interest and gravity. Very large concessions have been made to the Christian side by those who might have been expected, *à priori*, to have more sympathy with the depreciatory estimate of Judaism. No doubt candid and favourable judgments of Jesus have been passed before by Jews, as by Orobio, who speaks of Him as a "just and innocent man" (*vir justus et innocens*, p. 63); but the recent strain of commendation by unbelievers has been singular. Renan thus speaks of Him: "This sublime person, who daily presides still over the destiny of the world, we may call Divine, not in the sense that Jesus has absorbed all divinity or been (to speak scholastically) adequate to the idea, but in the sense that Jesus is the individual who has made His species take the greatest step towards the divine" (*Vie de Jésus*, p. 457). Thus also Strauss: "When Jesus exhorted His disciples to be perfect as their Father in heaven was, He thought of God in a moral point of view, as He found Himself affected in the loftiest moments of His own religious life, and by this ideal He strengthened His own religious life in turn. The deepest religious sentiment which lay in His consciousness was that all embracing love —the love that overcomes evil with good, which He accordingly transferred to God as the essence of His being. . . . . And when Jesus had developed in Himself this spirit which, joyfully one with God, embraced all men as brethren, He had realized in Himself the prophetic ideal of a new covenant along with the law written on the heart, Jer. xxxi. 31" (*Neues Leben Jesu*, p. 207). These writers, indeed, do not hold Jesus faultless, but they allow Him to have gone as near that point as human infirmity permitted, and the same concession is made by a well-known English writer of the freest school, Mr. Rathbone Greg: "I value the religion of Jesus, not as being absolute and perfect truth, but as containing more truth, purer truth, higher truth, stronger truth than has ever yet been given to man. Much of His teaching I unhesitatingly receive as to the best of my judgment unimprovable and unsurpassable, fitted, if obeyed, to make earth a Paradise indeed, and man only a little lower than the angels" (*Creed of Christendom*, p. 244). And again, "The spirituality of Christ's character, and the superhuman excellence of his life lie at the bottom of the dogma of the Incarnation" (p. 283).

It may be respectfully suggested to Jewish minds, that only a strong and overpowering excellence could have drawn forth these tributes from writers opposed to the divine origin and authority of Christianity; and it has to be added that the chief objections which they take to the absolute completeness of the moral character of Jesus, are removed by granting His Divine dignity; for the air of authority complained of as one fault, and a certain enthusiastic expectation of greater honours and results than fall to the lot of man or any creature, are, by this supposition of a higher, while at the same time inclusively human, personality, turned into harmonies and fitnesses. Could the assumption of the Divinity of Jesus be maintained, it is quite certain also that the Jewish charge of blasphemy would lose its force, and that the appearance of throwing life away would vanish; for not to mention that a good man is entitled, like the Maccabean martyrs, to sacrifice life for a good object, the superiority to ordinary laws of one whose life is self-dependent, must vindicate here for Jesus a more than mortal liberty. Nor can the natural prejudice of Jewish minds against the character of Jesus, as connected with a claim to enlarge and modify the religion of Moses, maintain itself, if the position be once looked at, that a higher, even a divine, prophet is not in the nature of things inconceivable; and that then the tone of authority, which sounds at first like arrogance, is a natural fitness and perfection; as Moses, had he returned to earth, would naturally have dwarfed all other prophets. To judge of Jesus here, and especially to annul all His other moral excellences, without attempting to enter into the Christian point of view, is hardly fair ; and a Christian would be guilty of the same unfairness were he to dismiss Mahomet without even looking at any real or alleged virtues or glories of character, that supported his pretensions. In this connexion the very patriotism of Jesus ; His tears shed over those who rejected Him ; His prayer for the authors of His death, "Father, forgive them; for they know not what they do ;" His command to His disciples, to begin the preaching of the good news, which He believed Himself called to seal by His blood, in Jerusalem, reveal a grandeur and depth of charity, which blend the extremes of earnestness and of tenderness, and attest, even by the highest Jewish standard, the calling of a prophet, and more than a prophet. It is the same to a Christian eye at every point of his moral career. Orobio admits (p. 63), that in denouncing the sins of the people and the hypocrisy of the rulers, He did no more than the Rabbis were bound to do in the synagogues every Sabbath-day ; and the courage which thus braved a worse death than any of the prophets, was in the track of their sufferings in its deepest spirit and motives; while His whole life was a going about doing good in ways which none of them organized into a daily labour. It is impossible to think of the humanity and gentleness of Christ without indignant repudiation in His name of the wrongs and cruelties, so long and shamefully inflicted by Christians upon the race for whom His image and memory ought to have secured not only recognition, but sympathy; yet what Christian heart has been so wounded by these injuries, as that of the loving Saviour Himself, who all through has been mourning over the stain thus cast upon His religion, and rebuking His persecuting disciples, who knew not what spirit they were of!

Is not this to a Jewish mind the most instructive lesson of the perfection of Jesus, that it avails at length to correct the errors alike of friends and foes, and that every great advance in mercy and in humility, as in truth and righteousness, is connected with His name? We have already the confession of Orobio, that if Christ's morality were practised, men would live like angels: but even as in Himself, so in those who follow Him, the morality cannot be disjoined from the doctrine; and as Christ can only shine in His true moral splendour when placed in the higher firmament of a Divine glory, so it is, as united with Him, and thus cleansed from sin, and impelled by that Divine Spirit whom He puts within them, that men and nations rise to the level of His calling. He needs to descend that He may rise and lift others with Him ; and this mystery of suffering and death for human salvation, as it gives the deepest consecration to His own moral greatness and tenderness, alone supplies the impulse to repentance, and the spring to a higher than natural virtue. If this career of a moral Reformer and Saviour is not stamped upon the life and work of Jesus Christ, first by His efforts of love and intercession with God, not to change His will but carry out His grace, and then by His sublime influence and example as an appeal to the hearts of men, Christians have wholly misread His history. But having felt this impulse, and felt it with a power and a blessedness denied to all besides, they may, nay, they must speak of it, and to Jew and to Gentile they must bear the testimony, "That which we have seen and heard declare we unto you, that ye also may have fellowship with us, and truly our fellowship is with the Father, and with His Son Jesus Christ."

This impression made by Christ's personal character, as revealed and standing unchallengeable in history, is something altogether unique. Socrates among the Greeks, Moses among the Hebrews, has drawn forth no such tributes, has been surrounded with no such wide and ever-growing veneration. How is it to be explained on the supposition that all is a mistake, or mere natural greatness exaggerated to Divine proportions? The Jew has here to bow to the voice of history, as he believes in the supernatural, and since the supernatural cannot be exhausted in one manifestation. If the Incarnation is not an impossibility, it may be a fact; and a fresh reading of the prophets may shew that prophecy too lends its witness, and that this wonderful life is written twice over, not only in Gospel records, but first of all and centuries before, in oracles like those which even an Ewald applies to a Messiah, the hope of Israel; and which even a Strauss, as in regard to the liii. of Isaiah, admits to be very hard to be turned away from a single person, and in which he grants that the mighty Sufferer read beforehand—with a sense of strength and consolation—what He took to be the inspired story of His own death as an anticipated atonement for the sins of many.

III. The third and last question connected with this historical wonder is, How came the historical success, prevalence, and influence of Christianity? This branches out into two parts—the success of Christianity, and the comparative failure of Judaism since the Christian era. And *first*, of the success of Christianity. No doubt Christianity has been only imperfectly successful. In the first ages it reached its limits in a few centuries; it was long torpid and stagnant, if not declining; and to this day it is but the religion of a minority of the human race. Other religions, too, have been successful in some sort—

Buddhism in China, Mahometanism both in the East and in the West—while ancient Rome, with all its tolerance, spread its gods, and especially the worship of the emperor, from the Euphrates to the Rhine. But with every abatement, Christianity has been the most successful religion in history, and, at this day, of all religions, rules in the intellectual and moral world. The gigantic systems of ancient paganism which it found in full possession of the centres of civilization, and which Judaism had done so little to eradicate, or even to assimilate to itself, Christianity in three or four centuries wholly swept away. Nor will it avail to account for this revolution, as Orobio does (p. 68), by the congeniality of a human God, dead, raised and seated on high, to Gentile conceptions; for the cross was to the Greek as great a scandal as to the Jew, and Christianity had to force its way by the arguments of innumerable apologists, and the blood of countless martyrs, and only in its victory relapsed into conformity with paganism. It created, even in its decay, the institutions of the middle ages, out of which modern Europe rose, and by which it is still fashioned. It revived with the revival of letters, shaking off its own corruptions, and in Protestantism coming nearer to Judaism in the best sense, and linking its future career with Bible study, with prophet-like earnestness of spirit, and with true and universal liberty. Of all religions Christianity is the only one that has carried through a successful Reformation, and that has stood its ground to this hour amidst the advancing tide of culture and even of unbelief, blessing the poor and the outcast with its inward consolations and immortal hopes; while owning no defeat in the sorest conflicts with sceptical philosophy, with materialistic science, and with the wild spirit of anarchy and revolution. It is identified in our own and in other lands with the progress of temperance; with the sacredness of chastity and domestic ties; and with the alliance between education and a pure and virtuous literature. In this one century it has abolished the slave-trade and burst the fetters of colonial slavery, emancipated the serfs of Russia, and overruled the most terrible of civil wars to the same merciful issue. It at once impels and makes tributary to itself every useful industry and healing art, writes its name upon colonization and discovery, and, by its missions in every land, binds itself up with the purpose of history and the unity of the world. These are but the outward victories of Christianity; its best conquests are in depths to which no eye of man can penetrate. When the heart is wrung with the sadness of remorse and fear, it recalls the "Man of sorrows," who found a remedy for sin in His own unutterable woe and solitude; it recovers the wanderer by the memory of the good Shepherd who gave His life for the sheep; amidst the sullen gloom of affliction it gives wing to prayer by the thought of that Intercessor whose own head was bowed in agony; and when the last parting comes it meets the mourner at the gate with words to which Death has already yielded—" I am the Resurrection and the Life!" So long as Christ can constrain the inmost spirits of men by spells like these, His religion is not a failure. It is on its way to a wider empire over everything that is not fatally hostile; and that earlier faith which before His day, as Christians believe, heralded its coming and its victories, has only departed from it for a season to be recovered for ever.

The second element of wonder is, that Christianity should have been advancing while Judaism is stationary or in comparative decay. Doubtless, the vitality of the Jewish race is wonderful. Its preservation is a miracle of history. Its resources, intellectual, commercial and political, are as fresh and inexhaustible as ever. It is not in these spheres that we speak of abated energy or influence. It is in the strictly religious sphere, where it comes most into contrast with the boundless vigour, the proselyting enthusiasm, the world-subduing spirit of Christianity. Where is there anything parallel in Jewish circles? Where anything even to equal the impulse which Judaism gave in its Alexandrine development before the Christian era, and by the circulation of the Septuagint over the Greek-speaking world? For generations Judaism, as a religious force, has been little more than conservative. It has neither opened its gates to the Gentile, nor witnessed, by an active and missionary propagandism, for the great doctrines anciently given it to hold up before the nations. If they have been taught the unity of God, it has been by Christian more than Jewish influence. If the Ten Commandments, with the Sabbath law in the heart of them (though in an altered form) have become the moral lesson-book of nations, it is because Christian voices have re-echoed the trumpet-sound by which they were first spoken. If the hallowed names of Abraham, and Isaac, and Jacob have gone to the antipodes, and entered into the devotions of cannibals recovered from infanticide and worse horrors to follow these patriarchs in the way of righteousness, it is because the books of the Old Testament, that instructed them, form a portion of the millions of copies, in two hundred tongues, scattered by other than Jewish hands. Whence is this—a fact so patent and so acknowledged, that the mention of it can give no offence? Nay, whence is it that the dearest and most sacred of Jewish memories have found other propagators more effectual than their first custodiers, so that the Christian readers of Moses, as an inspired man of God, far outnumber the Jewish; the Psalms are unspeakably more widely sung in the church than in the synagogue, and the Christian counterpart of the Passover leaves every way behind in diffusion the original celebration? Can it be that the God of Israel has employed aliens more largely for the memory of His wonders than His own children, as if the tribe of Joseph in dispersion had carried His name farther than the tribe of Judah, or as if the Samaritans had made the law of Moses a world-wide book, while the chosen seed retained it in a corner? How is it that at every point the Jew finds his ground pre-occupied and his associations disturbed? He is confronted by another, and yet not another—for he hears everywhere in Christian lands of Israel, of Zion, of Jerusalem, of David, of a great High-Priest and an endless sacrifice, and of a people that sat long in darkness coming to walk in the light of the Lord. Is it not that the Israel of God's covenant has a wider sense, or at least an earlier birth, than has been dreamt of; that the great words of Moses' song have been fulfilled, " Rejoice, ye *Goim*, with His people !" and that the Gentiles sooner than the eyes of Israel have beheld the change, have responded to the call, " Ye are the children of the living God"? Does not this look like the fulfilment of the early Christian hope, not to mention Old Testament foreshadowings, that the outcast Gentiles would for a season get the start, and Israel at length awake as these gathered home? O that the spreading light might reveal the already risen Sun, and that under His glad and glorious beams, cheering the sadness of dispersion, chasing the darkness of alienation, Jew and Gentile might embrace as brethren, careless who had been first, and who last, in hasting to the meeting-point, but alike returning to Zion with songs and everlasting joy! Yes, the common song is prepared, the song of penitence to both, of glorying to neither, as abased they lie in the dust before that sovereign word which binds Sinai and Calvary in one: "I will have mercy on whom I will have mercy, and will have compassion on whom I will have compassion:" and its strain is this, "Lo, this is our God; we have waited for Him, and He will save us; this is the Lord, we have waited for Him; we will rejoice and be glad in His salvation! O that this salvation of Israel were come out of Zion! When the Lord bringeth back the captivity of His people, Jacob shall rejoice and Israel shall be glad!" In the view of such a future, the desire of all nations, the fulness of the Messianic age, the common need and hope of Jew and Christian, struggling already through the sin and darkness of time and brightening to the glory of an eternal kingdom (which, O thou God of our fathers, grant that through thine own Messiah we all may share!) let us with one heart take up the prayers, "Look down from heaven, and behold from the habitation of Thy holiness and of Thy glory; where is Thy zeal and Thy strength, the sounding of Thy bowels and of Thy mercies towards me? are they restrained? Doubtless, Thou art our Father, though Abraham be ignorant of us and Israel acknowledge us not: Thou, O Lord, art our father, our Redeemer; Thy name is from everlasting." "Give ear, O Shepherd of Israel, Thou that leadest Joseph like a flock, Thou that dwellest between the cherubim, shine forth. Before Ephraim, and Benjamin and Manasseh stir up Thy strength and come and save us. Turn us again, O God, and cause Thy face to shine and we shall be saved!" "Let Thy hand be upon the man of Thy right hand, the Son of man whom Thou madest strong for Thyself. So will not we go back from Thee; quicken us and we will call upon Thy name. Turn us again, O Lord God of hosts, cause Thy face to shine and we shall be saved." Amen.

II.

Christianity, the Justification of the Mosaic Economy.

BY

REV. CANON COOK, M.A.

II.

CHRISTIANITY, THE JUSTIFICATION OF THE MOSAIC ECONOMY.

WHEN we consider the early history of mankind, specially that portion in which our race attained its highest development, one name stands out in unrivalled pre-eminence. It is the name of the man who first promulgated the central truths of all religion in a form which has impressed itself indelibly upon the conscience of humanity; who first instituted a political system resting on the basis of law in the place of individual will; who declared the principles on which all sound morality depends, and that in a code equally remarkable for simplicity and completeness; who in his own life exemplified the principles which he inculcated, not as his own discovery, but as derived by a personal communication from the eternal source of light and life; the name of the first and most original of historians, legislators, patriots, prophets, and divines,—the name of the Hebrew Moses.

The facts are indeed such as cannot but excite the

deepest feelings of interest and curiosity. If we look at them as they are recorded in the narrative of the Pentateuch, fully and faithfully, as the truest representatives of Hebrew and of Christian thought have ever held; if even we set aside all contested points, confining ourselves to circumstances which, as all admit, must underlie the narrative, we have results of transcendent and unquestioned importance,—results, be it noted, accomplished by the instrumentality of one man, unaided, and, indeed, from first to last thwarted by those among whom and for whom he worked. Wherever we find a recognition of the unity and absolute supremacy of God ; wherever we find the religion which, whatever may be its other claims, is, at present, unquestionably co-extensive with all true civilization, which is professed by all nations which recognise the mutual rights and obligations of men, and alone for some ages have advanced and are still advancing in every department of science and art, there we find, fair and full in proportion to the stage of mental and moral development, a recognition of the principles established in the Mosaic dispensation, of the position of Moses as foremost among the early teachers of the world.

When, indeed, the Pentateuch was first brought into contact with the Gentile mind, clothed by the Alexandrians in the language of Greece, it took its place at once among the chief factors of progressive thought. The originality, the grandeur of its first utterances were discerned by the profoundest critics; philanthropists and legislators found in it a new source for the elucidation of fundamental principles of right. Late inquiries have shown that shortly before the Christian period, its influence, indirectly and unconsciously, but rapidly, pervaded the religious and philosophic atmosphere of the ancient world. Nor when under a new form—a form, as we hold, distinctly foreshadowed or intimated in the narrative—the inmost principles of the Pentateuch, divested of all merely local and temporal associations, in their highest energy and perfect development achieved the conquest over heathenism in the fairest regions of Europe and Asia, was the great name of the author eclipsed, or obscured. If indeed you would look out for the fullest appreciation of the genius, the principles, the influence of the Hebrew legislator, you will find it, not, as might perhaps be expected, in the early Rabbinical writings, nor even in the works of the noble and lofty spirits of mediæval Judaism, or of the worthiest representatives of Israel in our own time; but in the writings of large-hearted and earnest Christians, who see in every triumph of their religion a continuation of his work, in every discovery of Divine truth a development of his principles. A new light is indeed cast upon that noble countenance seen through the medium of Christianity. The cross, with its antecedents and results, does not stand out in antagonism to Sinai. It alone explains, and in explaining it alone justifies, the code with all its concomitants, its multifarious and mysterious institutions, which were there committed to Moses. It tells us for what purposes they were given, it teaches their necessity and their use; and no man accepts all the claims of Moses to our admiration and reverence so unreservedly and gratefully as he to whom the cross is dearest, who sees in it, and in it only, the pledge of the redemption of man.

This is indeed the point which I am specially called upon to bring before you. The full explanation, and therefore the full and the only real justification, of the Mosaic dispensation, is to be found in the fulfilment of all that it promised or prefigured by the Christ; for whose coming every true Israelite was ever looking forward; by whose coming, as every true Christian believes, salvation has been made attainable to every individual of the human race.

Here, however, on the outset I am met by the obvious objection: If the character and work of Moses be such as I have described, how can I speak of the need of any explanation, more specially of any justification? To this I answer, the whole question is, in what light are we to look on that character or that work? Is the system as it stands in the Pentateuch to be regarded as complete and final—the last word of God to man? Or is it to be regarded as a preparatory dispensation, a necessary stage in the progressive revelation of the Divine will, and as such of necessity incomplete, its true glory being derived from what it prefigured, and for which it paved the way? The former is the Jewish, the latter the Christian point of view. The Jewish view is stated clearly by the most authoritative exponents of Judaism. These are the words of Maimonides in the ninth chapter of his treatise on the fundamentals of the law:—" It is declared and expounded in the law that its every precept standeth fast for all generations; that in it there is no place for any variation—nothing can be taken from it, nothing can be added to it." This principle, which in the Bible applies to the immutable moral and spiritual law, is thus extended to the whole Mosaic system. All prophets and inspired writers had but one work—to determine the application of unvarying truths to ever-varying circumstances. Indeed, the whole of the prophetical books—those books in which the voice of God sounds to us and to the Israelite so grandly—were regarded as destined to pass away; eternity was reserved to the Pentateuch alone, which was to retain its position as the source and substance of all revealed truth, even in the Messianic time.* Some modern advocates of Judaism, as opposed to Christianity, tell us that

* The passage is curious. In the "Hilcoth Megilla" Maimonides says:—"All the books of the Prophets, and all the Cetubim (sc. Hagiographi) are to be abolished in the days of Messiah, except the history of Esther."

we are to judge of the code and institutions of the Pentateuch with reference to later expositions; but the older and more influential rabbis taught that attempts to explain its injunctions, to develop its principles, are presumptuous, and utterly uncalled for. Moses, according to them, alone saw God face to face, received into his own mind and communicated to others all that could be revealed of the Divine will. That was the essential distinction between all other prophets and Moses—they saw in shadow, in enigma, through a veil or a glass darkly, and prophesied in dream, or ecstasy, or vision; God revealed to him what no man knew before him, or saw after him. Hence the Talmud holds "that Messiah must be the greatest of future prophets, as being nearest in spirit to our master Moses." Now, I hold that position to be absolutely untenable; it is, in fact, though tacitly, yet really abandoned by the ablest Jewish writers themselves; there is no precept, no institution peculiar to Mosaism which does not undergo a complete transformation in order to bring it into conformity with the developed intelligence of man. In fact, if we examine the distinctive principles and institutions of Mosaism, without reference to their bearings upon higher truths, afterwards to be revealed, we shall find them incapable of justification in some points of most serious importance; a retrograde even rather than an onward movement is demonstrable. They stand out in unfavourable contrast to the religion and principles of the patriarchs as described by Moses himself, whether we regard their forms of worship, their family life, or their relations to the world without. But on the other hand, when we look into those institutions and examine that code, with reference to what was to follow them, we recognise their full significance and grandeur; we see in them a real and necessary stage in the progressive revelation of the Divine will: bringing all that preceded them up to the point of culmination; causing the need of a future disclosure to be intensely realized; taking man in a state of immature development; keeping him for a season in a state of subjection and training; exercising faculties for which full scope would be afterwards given; thus doing their proper work as the best conceivable παιδαγωγός, guide, protector, and tutor, until he was fit for admission into the school of Christ.

It is evident that it would take a long time to work out this proposition. I can only hope to throw out a few suggestions, which those who are interested in the subject may follow up at their leisure; nor do I fear that the imperfect form in which they are necessarily presented will entirely obscure the great truths which, if received, would complete the reconciliation of God's ancient people with the followers of their own Christ.

First let us consider the form of religion, specially of religious worship as it was settled by the Mosaic code. Was it, regarded by itself, an advance? Could it have been intended to be permanent? Here the means of forming a tolerably correct judgment are at hand. We have the earlier forms of religious service depicted by the same master hand which sets before us the multifarious and imposing ceremonial of the Israelites. Both are brought into immediate juxtaposition in successive books; and certainly no greater contrast can well be conceived than that which comes before us in two of these books, the one dealing with the period before Moses, the other detailing the institutions which Moses was commanded to establish. It would make no substantial difference in this argument were we even to allow weight to the assertions of those critics who assume that the two books, Genesis and Leviticus, not to speak of Exodus, belong to different authors, and to different times. No one questions that the former book presents the only portraiture, no candid and well-informed reader doubts that it presents a singularly vivid and faithful portraiture of the patriarchal times, or that the latter gives a no less faithful account of the Mosaic institutions. That Moses wrote both is my own conviction, that which has been, till within the last hundred years, the general, the all but universal belief among Jews and Christians; but whether he wrote both or not, it is certain that in both we find the only account of the great facts which he received and taught.

In the former book let us confine our attention to the form of religion as presented to Abraham. No personage in the Old Testament stands out more distinctly before us. He is, indeed, the very first person in the world's history with whom we seem to have a personal acquaintance. Other forms are there with clear, definite outlines,—nothing, indeed, is more remarkable than the vivid impression which the inspired historian makes by a few plain words as he brings before us the ancestors of our race. But in Abraham we see a friend; we note the movements of a kindred heart; his words and thoughts find a response in our mind. We revert naturally to him when we would touch the chord of religious emotion, when we would see how a noble and loving spirit would approach its God. Now, of all characteristics of the religion of Abraham, the most striking is its thorough personality. In prayer, in every act of religious worship, his soul is in direct contact with its object. God speaks to his spirit, his spirit addresses God, without any intervention. Abraham knows indeed of the existence of a priesthood: he recognises the position and claims of Melchizedek; but for himself, for his family, he feels no need of such an institution: it did not belong to the inner sphere of communion with God. Sacrifices he offers on certain occasions, but they do not enter into his daily life, and they are offered by his own hands, not in a temple, but under the open vault of heaven; offered as the expression of a heart devoting itself, and all that it loves and prizes, unreservedly to God. Such was the religion of Abraham, such was the religious worship of all the Patriarchs,—each father in his own household discharging the simple but most significant offices of the priesthood, each drawing near to God without any burdensome or elaborate ceremonial, each receiving from God personal marks of acceptance. Nor is this true only of the head of each family. The wife, the children, the dependents, live in habits of direct communion with a Father ever accessible, ever willing to receive and to answer their prayers. The religious life had free play. Certainly the limits within which it was called forth were somewhat narrow. The problems which surge up from the depths of thought perplexed by the mysteries of the material and the spiritual universe did not come within its scope. The relations between the Almighty and vast communities remained to be discovered or revealed; but still there we have in principle and potentiality an exemplar which, fully developed and applied, comes exceedingly near to the ideal of a living intercourse between God and man.

Turn from this to the Israelite under the Levitical

code. What we first note is the separation of the nation into diverse and strongly contrasted classes. The elements of religious life, which hitherto had been harmoniously combined in the patriarchal family, were now violently and permanently disjoined. On the one side a priesthood remarkable, even when compared with the priesthood of other nations, for the completeness of its isolation ; hereditary, transmitted from father to son, irrespective of personal qualifications ; a priesthood carefully shielded from ceremonial impurity by avoidance of all contact with those without, commanded to abstain from demonstrations of natural affection in times which draw out man's deepest and tenderest feelings ; a priesthood marked out by striking accessories, personal and official, performing the most sacred offices, those which most nearly concerned the spiritual life of the people, in a part of a sanctuary inaccessible to all others, spending the greater portion of their own lives in duties which, notwithstanding all that can be said as to their significance, must have been wearisome to the last degree ; duties, in fact, which might seem in some respects suitable only to persons of coarse habits and blunted senses; foremost among them being the sacrificial rites when the blood of unnumbered victims dyed the marble pavement, when the courts of the temple echoed with the moans of beasts expiring under the priestly blows. Taken as the last, the highest representative of man, permitted to worship his Maker, we cannot but look upon the Levitical priest with amazement,—such amazement as Abraham might be conceived to have felt had the Levitical service been presented to his spirit in vision, had he seen the mass of his own descendants—a people in covenant with God—shut out from the priest's court, the high priest isolated from his brethren, forbidden himself to enter the sanctuary and approach the mercy-seat save on one solemn occasion, when above all points the most striking was the intimation of a fearful chasm between God and man. We seem to hear the great Patriarch, the father of the faithful, say, What beggarly elements are these? What strange superstition? What is become of the promises? Where is the adoption? Are these my children? Are these the children of God? Abraham, in fact, once fully assured that all this ceremonial, with its countless details, was actually appointed by God Himself, must have been driven to one of two alternatives: either that his descendants were so degenerate, so lost to spiritual truths, that they were incapable of the communion to which he was himself admitted, in which he found the source of spiritual life,—an alternative in which it was scarcely possible for him to acquiesce, though I may observe in passing, it has at various times been maintained not only by some Christian thinkers but by writers of great authority among the Hebrews themselves;—

or Abraham would take the other and the true alternative,—all these forms pointed to realities hereafter to be revealed; they foreshadowed some great truths of eternal significance, they were intended to awaken the spiritual sense, and to prepare it for a spiritual manifestation, for the coming of One who would satisfy all wants of the human heart. It was simply impossible that what was then presented to the outer sense should be the ultimate form of a religion which has for its special and, indeed, its only object, the entire restoration of union with God.

And let me ask you, who know anything of the history and writings of those descendants of Abraham, who have not accepted the realization in Christ, of all promises and foreshadowings, has not such been more or less consciously a general feeling among them? The temple, the priesthood, the altar of sacrifice, the whole Levitical ceremonial, have long since past away; Israelites have no substitute for them. Regarding them, as they undoubtedly were, the most prominent, in fact the essential characteristics of the Mosaic system, they can with difficulty prove themselves to be still true Jews: subject, indeed, to the law, so far as regards its penalties, but without its atonements; bound by enactments with which they know it is impossible to comply. We might expect one long wail for the loss of what were once regarded, and are still formally represented, to have been the most glorious privileges of the chosen race. And doubtless the loss is inwardly felt; there is a profound melancholy in the devoutest works of the devoutest Hebrews. Longings for the past, aspirations for the future, call forth our deepest and tenderest sympathy as we listen to the supplications and hymnody of the synagogue; but after all it is true that the restoration of the Temple service, of all the ceremonial of the Levitical code, is far from being to them the main object of desire. It would, in fact, be a terrible incumbrance to them. Their ablest teachers are well aware, and they are disposed to triumph in the fact, that the doctor has taken the place of the priest, the teacher of the sacrificer. For the service of the Temple they recognise a not inadequate substitute in the service of the synagogue—an intermediate service between that of the Mosaic institution and that of the Christian Church; differing from both inasmuch as it is without the sacramental foreshadowings of the one and the sacramental representations of the other, and as such essentially inferior to both in significance and effect, but which after all they feel comes nearer to the reasonable service which man is bound to offer to his God than that external form, when divested of the prophetic significance to which alone it owed its worth. I ask, how is it that the learned, the devout, the powerful, the opulent community of the Hebrews remains satisfied in a condition so hardly to be reconciled with their religious principles? Is it not a proof that the most influential of their leaders, nay, that the great mass of the people, have ceased to long really for the restoration of the temple? And if so, does not this prove that they are inwardly conscious that the Mosaic code in its literal sense and outward observances belongs to the past? Strangely enough we do sometimes hear of the reconstruction of the Temple, of the restoration of the old ritual, the re-establishment of the priesthood with all ceremonial forms as a thing in itself desirable, and to be looked for as a concomitant of the restoration of the Hebrews to their old homes; but, so far as I am aware, such speculations have little vogue among the Hebrews themselves; at least I find scarcely any indications of them in the writings of their chief teachers; they occur chiefly, if not exclusively, in the expositions of prophetical sayings by some Christians, who seeing, and that very rightly, in all those divinely appointed forms figures and representations of the work and person of Christ, most unreasonably, as I think, would have us look forward to their restoration.

What we feel—I speak now in the name of the great body of my fellow-Christians—is that all those rites and forms, the sacrifices, the altar, the temple, the priesthood, were full of meaning, and that they were instituted at the right time, that they did their appointed work; they were according to the pattern shown to Moses on the mount; presenting to the eye of sense, and through that sense to the awakened conscience, what the greatest of prophets saw with the spiritual sense. In the exclusion of the people from the sacred courts we read the judgment of God on sin, its unspeakable defilement, its inevitable condemnation, the separation from God which it necessarily involves, and which must continue until it has been expiated; in the representation of the high priest we have a singularly complete bodying forth of the ideal of One in whom the reunion of God and man should be complete, at once one with God and one with man, a true Mediator, not as distinct from both, but as inseparable from both, the righteousness of God being satisfied, the sin of man being put away. The first Christian teachers dwell lovingly upon each significant detail, realizing the absolute identity of the truths which underlay the whole system of Moses with those revealed in the person of Messiah: and here I may express my own confident hope that fuller, clearer, and more critical expositions may be looked for when many descendants of the chosen race —a race specially remarkable for keenness and depth of spiritual instinct—come among us, not as strangers, but as our elder brethren, restored to their rightful place among the subjects of their Christ.

From the forms of worship I pass to the legislation. Here I admit that it stands out conspicuous for principles of the highest value, partially recognised or wholly ignored in all other ancient codes. No legislation ever kept the balance between private and public duty so justly. The claims of the state were as in all codes paramount, yet here in this code, and here alone, with due regard to the rights of individuals. Each family preserved its own integrity, domestic affections held their own place, not trampled upon as elsewhere when competing with national interests. The wife, the mother had a far higher place than that assigned to her in the great Aryan communities most remarkable for their civilization. The child, though subject to the parent, was not, as among the Romans, his slave or chattels. The servant himself differed essentially from the slave of Gentile peoples; he was a member of the family; whether Hebrew or alien by race he was admitted to all the privileges of religious worship, no distinction being made between him and the child of the family in the holiest rites. Large as were the powers of the owner, they were strictly defined and limited by law. I gladly accept all that has been eloquently urged by Salvador in his great work on the Institutions of Moses. Regarded as a stage in man's progress, we recognise a mighty advance. We have, in fact, the very first instance in the history of the world of an organized community living on terms of absolute equality before God, without a despot, without an oligarchical caste, governed wholly by law; nor can we think without admiration of the man who, having the whole disposition of affairs in his own hand, made no special place of rank and power for his own descendants, and effectually excluded the descendants of his brother from the secular position which, in conjunction with the priesthood, has created and perpetuated the most formidable despotisms known to the world.

But all this rests on the assumption that we are contemplating a stage in human progress under Divine guidance; not a completion. Nothing can be fairer than the defence on this ground of regulations which now jar painfully on our feelings, which, were they maintained as the last word of God, would be simply unendurable. The people was to be kept together as a distinct nation. It was necessary that all relations, external and internal, should be settled with reference to that condition. The laws which defined their relations must needs be such as would be intelligible to the people in their actual state of mind and feelings—their observance must be practicable; and this involved a certain amount of accommodation, of regard to temporary and mutable circumstances, an accommodation of which the proper limits are discernible by the highest wisdom, but which necessarily implies a partial application, nay, an apparent ignoring, of the absolute principles of right and justice,—such, in fact, as can only be justified by reference to an ultimate object, to be achieved by the separation of Israel from all surrounding nations. These observations apply to other points of high importance, to the relations between husband and wife, the toleration of easy divorce, to the relations between citizens, and very specially to the laws of retributive justice, to the recognition of the right of revenge. But the point which most needs justification, for which no justification can be found save that of temporary and peculiar preparation for a work important to all future races, is the bearing of the Mosaic legislation upon the feelings and conscience of the whole nation in reference to a vast sphere of moral duties. The special circumstances of the Israelites involved a total, though temporary, suspension of the principles of international law. Other nations were on terms of varying feeling towards their neighbours,—hostile for the most part it is true, yet often indifferent, and sometimes friendly; those most bitterly opposed were not separated by fundamental principles, save in isolated cases which belong to a later period ; but the Israelites were to be absolutely apart, at open undying enmity with those idolatrous nations with which they were necessarily brought into closest contact. Feelings which now exist between nations at war with each other, specially Christian nations, could not be encouraged, or even tolerated. It was a tremendous condition attached to the necessary isolation of the people; one which presents a most unfavourable contrast to the condition of their great ancestors, one which Moses must have felt could only be imposed with a view to its entire abrogation when the purposes for which it was imposed should be fulfilled.

Look indeed at the contrast. Abraham and his descendants lived among heathens, keeping aloof from their superstitions, yet on terms of friendly intercourse; Abraham recognised in the chieftain of a Canaanitish tribe a real priest of the Most High God (Gen. xiv. 12): a principle which was fully accepted by Moses both in his writings and in the case of his own wife's father and brother, yet one of which all traces disappear after the promulgation of the law. The marriage of Joseph with the daughter of the priest of On is recorded without any intimation that it was displeasing to God or offensive to his own family when they joined him. The Egyptians indeed are described as shrinking from contact with Joseph's brethren, but no corresponding feeling is noted in their case, or in that of the two patriarchs who visited Egypt previously. But from the time of Moses to that of the Apostles it was the most prominent characteristic of Israelites; it has been the main cause of mutual repulsion between them and all Gentiles; and we must never forget that it came in with the institution of the ceremonial law. It answered its purpose thoroughly. It raised a barrier between the Jew and the Gentile insurmountable so long as that law should be outwardly observed; until, its object being secured, it should be withdrawn. War raging without truce or term became the normal state between the Israelite and those who in the mind of God, declared to the great forefather of the Hebrews, recorded by the legislator himself, were destined to be partakers of all the blessings. We look in vain for any justification of this state of hostility in the Old Testament, apart from its future results. We cannot indeed but feel that it implied a state of deplorable weakness in the Hebrew; it implied that he was so accessible to temptation that he could only be preserved from idolatry, the deadliest of all sins, by complete isolation; a child under a jealous tutor, kept, so to speak, in quarantine lest he should contract infection. But what a strange contrast to his true destiny! He was called to be the teacher, the light-bearer, the converter of the world, the firstborn among God's children, the instrument by which in God's own time the work of man's redemption from sin, from ignorance, from death was to be accomplished. What was he then, what is he now, so long as he remains in that isolation? He presented indeed, and still presents, a type of character which in important points commands respect and admiration, rising far above the highest standards of Gentilism. In religion a pure Monotheist, utterly aloof from the superstitions of heathendom on the one hand, and, on the other, from the baseless speculations and materialistic tendencies of Gentile philosophy. In domestic relations singularly pure, and remote alike from an unnatural asceticism and from the sensuality which disgraced the most civilized and intellectual races of the Old World. Towards the poor, the afflicted, ever compassionate, charitable to an extent not surpassed, and not often equalled, by any people. In truth a high and noble character, one which stands out grandly through the various vicissitudes of national history, whether we look at the Jews in their own land, or in their dispersion, under Persians, Greeks, Romans, Mahometans, or Christians, but withal a character in one respect apart—apart and incomplete exactly to the extent of his adherence to the old law, of his rejection of its highest and truest bearings; wanting one qualification, and one only—entire sympathy with man as man, a sympathy resting on the recognition of man's inherent and inalienable relation to God, developed by the work of Christ. It was because the law formed such men as the Apostles, whom we recognise at once as Hebrews of the Hebrews, and as our own leaders, that we see its complete justification; but only because those men realized and accomplished their true vocation as heralds of salvation to mankind.

Another point on which the law of Moses specially needs the justification which it finds in the Gospel—a proof indeed that it was not, and could not be intended to be, the final revelation of God's will—is the extent and character of its omissions. I can but touch on this point very briefly, but must not pass it over unnoticed. The most striking omission is that of a distinct and authoritative revelation of a future state. Now there are good reasons why this should not have formed part of a merely temporary law. That law had to deal with outward acts. Its sanctions, its penalties were temporal; it dealt with man in every state and condition; it taught him that he was under the government of one from whom no act or thought could be concealed, that the judgment was certain and immediate. A great thinker found in this limitation a strong evidence of the supernatural character of the Mosaic dispensation; but it certainly is a conclusive evidence of its incompleteness. Within the sphere of political, social, ceremonial life there was light, sufficient to guide every movement; without that sphere there was an infinite blank, so far as the law was concerned. Now sufficient reason may be alleged for the omission, provided that it was for a season only. The subject could not be dealt with in a Divine revelation at all, if it were not dealt with thoroughly. A future state involves a future judgment, and the conditions of that judgment, specially as regards the punishment of sin, could not be fully declared until the terms on which pardon is attainable should be revealed. In fact, the announcement of expiation by the sacrifice, which all other sacrifices prefigured, was a necessary preliminary for the revelation of eternal life. Observe, this applies only to the Mosaic dispensation, to the written code. The ancestors of the Hebrews lived in sure hope of another state, and ever spoke of themselves as sojourners on earth, exiles from their true home. They felt, though they may not have drawn out the thought in express words, that the soul living to God must live to Him for ever. In truth had they not lived in that conviction they would have had less light than the Gentiles. We find the belief in a state after death a prominent characteristic in every ancient religious system. In Egypt, the people best known to Moses and his brethren, it may almost be said that the present life had no significance but as a preparatory stage towards reunion with the Deity: every act, every thought was to be examined after death, and to receive exact and full recompense. But the light which shone on the minds of early saints was not held up, as might be expected, by the great teacher of the Hebrews to his people. The only imaginable justification for this is surely that it was necessarily reserved for the coming Revealer. The state of the Hebrew mind in the meantime is strangely interesting, and without a clear perception of its bearings it is somewhat perplexing. A deep gloom rested at times upon noble spirits. There are passages in the effusions of the devoutest and deepest thinkers which make us feel that they were passing through the valley of the shadow of death. Upon lower carnal minds the effect was deadening. The evil liver, the sensualist, the secularist, found in the omission a relief from all fear of responsibility in the future. But on the other hand,—and this is the main point to which I would bespeak your attention,—the withholding of the light wrought powerfully upon noble spirits. The yearnings of the heart created in God's image could not rest unsatisfied. A deep, intense faith, deeper and more intense in the absence of external support, was developed,—a faith not, as some will have it, derived from alien sources, not, properly speaking, the outcome of the Mosaic law, but resting on intimations of the Divine work in the Mosaic record of older times, and heartily received by all true Hebrews. Towards the close of the national career, nay, before the struggles of the Maccabean period, belief fully developed, and that in the form recognised by Christianity, belief in the immortality of man, in the continuance and perfect restoration of his personal identity, was become the special and distinctive characteristic of the true Hebrew. What the belief needed was a pledge, a proof, an authoritative assurance of its truth, such an assurance as was afforded by the resurrection of our Lord.

In concluding this incomplete, but, I fear, tedious attempt to deal with a great subject, let me revert briefly to a hope which has found expression more than once in my address. It lies very near to my heart. I speak of the hope that many true Israelites will ere long be found among the ablest champions of the cross, the faithful soldiers of their own Messiah. It is certain that if they join us they will find all the claims of their own forefathers heartily recognised. · No words will they hear from Christians in disparagement of the patriarchs, the prophets—the great representatives of Israel. They will find us earnestly and lovingly studying the words which sound most powerfully in their own hearts. They will have nothing to unlearn which they have drawn from their own scriptures; what they have to learn will be but a development of their most precious points of faith. That the mass of the people will join us in a period within the range of human foresight is perhaps not to be hoped for, much as it is to be desired. Much must be done before the Church of Christ is in a state which would justify the expectation : but there is no reason to doubt that here and there one, nay, very many, certainly not the weakest or lowest spirits will be attracted to the Cross. They have had precursors in all ages. In the tenth century Ibn Gebirol, known in Europe as Avecebron, influenced the forms of theological thought among the greatest schoolmen ; in the twelfth, Maimonides, a man recognised by Hebrew and by Gentile as one of the master-spirits of the world, was acknowledged as a fellow, not to say teacher, by the mighty intellect of Thomas Aquinas; and the works of both have lately been brought into stronger light than heretofore by the labour of one of the greatest scholars and thinkers of our own time, but lately deceased, the Hebrew Munk. Looking at the indirect, unconscious tendency of their writings, chiefly intent on reconciling science with religion, we may safely assert that the profoundest thinkers among them have come very near us. Many indeed have come among us. One great school especially (I speak of the masters of the Cabbala) came so near to us as to rouse excessive and not unreasonable alarm among the upholders of the national traditions. They were persons whose minds influenced very powerfully some of the leading spirits at the time of the great Reformation I speak of Ricci, the physician of the Emperor Maximilian; of Leo the Hebrew, the gifted son of a gifted father, Abarbanel; and others, whose works were eagerly studied by such men as Reuchlin, Mirandola, and many devout and large-hearted Christians. Nor is our own age without examples. We count indeed among our clergy more than one hundred Hebrews, to a great extent occupied in missionary work. Germany has produced a vast array of Hebrew scholars, distinguished in every department of literature science, and art: foremost. among philologians—Benfey, Fuerst, Bernstein, Bernays, and Delitzsch, one of the soundest, ablest, and most learned expositors of Holy Scriptures ; great among historians—Jost, Grätz, Weil, and above all the Christian Neander, of all Church historians the most candid, genial, and devout, the man of widest and tenderest sympathies ; nor can we pass without a tribute of gratitude and admiration the warm-hearted genius who has given the fullest expression to the devout feelings of Christians in strains of unparalleled beauty and grandeur, Felix Mendelssohn ;—these and others may be named as instances of what may be expected from Hebrews retaining all the zeal, energy, religious instinct, special mental and moral qualifications of the race, and combining with them hearty allegiance to the Hebrew of Hebrews, the Man of men, the Completer of all revelation, the Mighty God, the Everlasting Father, the Prince of Peace. A long period of preparation preceded His first coming, during which many a great light shone forth among the Hebrews ; a still longer period has elapsed, during which the people have done no small work in transmitting the light of lofty thought from east to west and west to east ; may the time be near when they will take once more their true place among those who will prepare mankind for His second coming, and justify all that their own legislator did and said as the servant of their God.

III.
The Relation of the Jews to their own Scriptures.

BY THE

REV. PROFESSOR STANLEY LEATHES, M.A.

III.

THE RELATION OF THE JEWS TO THEIR OWN SCRIPTURES.

IF one were asked to specify the oldest historic people in the world, one could have little hesitation in naming the Jews. It is possible that the continuous existence of the Chinese may reach back for a yet longer period, but this can hardly be said of their historic existence; while the remoteness and comparative seclusion of the Chinese people may be regarded as exempting them from competition for the palm of national antiquity. When we speak of the oldest historic people in the world we naturally think of those nearer home who have a recognisable existence in the present and a definite and distinct historic existence in the past. Compared, for example, with ancient Rome, the Jewish nation may boast of a venerable and hoary antiquity. Suppose we accept the date 754 B.C. as that beyond which no actual existence can be assigned to Rome; then that date carries us but a very little way back in the history of

Israel—only to the era of some of her greatest kings and prophets. She was then in the fulness of her strength and maturity, when we can barely discern the very earliest commencements of the foundation of Rome. Or if we turn to Greece, and take the first Olympiad as our starting-point in 776 B.C., we find ourselves in the grayest and earliest dawn of Grecian national life. Draco flourished in the thirty-ninth Olympiad, Solon in the forty-sixth; the first Messenian war was 743, and the battle of Marathon, with which the long line of national glories may be almost said to begin, was more than 250 years later, or 490 B.C. But the same period brings us within a little to the close of the first great epoch of Jewish history as comprised in the records of the national sacred literature. The kingdom of Israel had come to an end more than two centuries before. Judah had been carried captive to Babylon more than one. The second Temple had already been built and dedicated some twenty-five or thirty years. The generation of old men who had wept when its foundation was laid must now have slept with their fathers, and the generation of younger men who on the same occasion had shouted for joy had already arrived at middle and mature age, or were feeble and gray-headed.

But this comparison has reference only to the past. Of historic Greece and Rome it may be truly said that they once were. As national entities they have no continuous existence reaching down to the present. The liveliest imagination can scarcely recognise in the modern kingdoms of Greece or Italy anything more than the successors of the old republics. There is nothing answering to continuity or identity of national existence.

But with Israel it is widely different. Her national existence is as distinct and well defined in the era of the Maccabees as in the time of Zerubbabel or Hezekiah; in the time of Christ as in the era of the Maccabees; in the middle ages, though under circumstances vastly modified, as in the first century of the Christian era; and in the present day as in the middle ages.

Physiologists tell us that the characteristics of race are among the most permanent and ineffaceable of all; but I question very much whether in all the annals of ethnology any other instance can be produced that bears any true analogy to the permanence and ineffaceable characteristics of the Jewish nation, whether any other people can point to a continuity of national existence so marked and undeniable as that of the Jews. For we must bear in mind that there is this great difference between the Chinese and the Jews, that though you may know a Chinaman whenever you see him, as you may know a Jew, yet the Chinaman has a home and a country, while the Jew has none,—has none, that is, peculiar to him as a Jew; for the Jew cannot be said to be any more at home in Palestine than he is in London. There is no country on the face of the world where you would at once say, "This is the natural home of the Jews; here they are indigenous, and here they constitute the bulk of the existing population." Whereas if you go to China it will at once be obvious that though you may have met with many Chinamen in various parts of the world, yet there you have traced them to their natural and original home. The continuity, therefore, of the Chinese nation, so far as it has had a continuous national existence, has been intimately bound up with their national localisation in China. But with the race of Israel it is very different. For the long period of eighteen centuries, at least, it cannot at any time have been said, that they were indigenous or peculiar to any one country in the world. And yet they have never at any time become mingled with, or absorbed in, the particular people or nation among whom they have lived. Their home is everywhere, and yet nowhere. They are to be found in every nation under heaven, and yet they are a distinct and separate people of themselves.

It is perfectly certain that no other instance can be produced exactly parallel to theirs. The Negro or the Mongol presents the characteristics of race sufficiently marked, but in a few generations they become entirely obliterated, and though we can speak of the Negro or Mongolian race we cannot speak of the Negro or Mongolian nation. Their individuality is more conspicuous than that of the Jew, but their nationality is much less so ; in fact it has no existence whatever. And this arises from the circumstance that their peculiarities of race run up to a period prior to all history, and have no special connection with history. Whereas in the case of the Jew his existence from first to last is an historic existence. No other person than Abraham has ever been regarded as the first father of the nation, and he it was who was first known as Abram the Hebrew. Attempts have recently been made to treat the times of Abraham as mythical, but these are only to be regarded as symptomatic of an age that is impatient of anything like traditional opinion and is wildly enamoured of speculation for its own sake. And with respect to them it is sufficient now to say that if these records are to be treated as mythical then the world possesses no ancient records, not to say no records at all that can justly be considered as history. And such a position is critically suicidal, because the very foundations are undermined upon which alone it becomes possible to base our proposed reconstruction of history. Though Abraham, however, is justly to be regarded as the first individual in whom the Jewish nation existed in form, and though there is probably no other nation that can point to a first original so certain or so well defined, yet we must not forget that properly speaking there was no *national* existence of the people in patriarchal times. The grandson of Abraham was the first that bore the name of Israel, and though he and his fathers seem to have been regarded as strangers and sojourners by the people among whom they dwelt, and to have possessed a kind of *family* nationality, yet it was not till centuries later that the existence of the *nation* definitely began. And in this respect the history of Israel presents the same marked contrast to that of other nations as it does in other respects. If we speak of ancient Rome or Greece, it becomes very difficult to say when the national existence of either one or the other first began. But with Israel we can put our finger upon the very month and day and hour. It was at midnight, on the fourteenth day of that memorable first month, when "the Lord smote all the firstborn in the land of Egypt, ... and there was a great cry in Egypt, for there was not a house where there was not one dead,"[1]—"this is that night of the Lord to be observed of all the children of Israel in their generations."[2] "And it came to pass the selfsame day that the Lord did bring the children of Israel out of the land of Egypt by their armies."[3] On that day a people six hundred thousand strong, who had before no national existence, but only the exist-

[1] Exodus xii. 29, 30.   [2] Exodus xii. 42.   [3] Exodus xii. 51.

ence of slaves in the hands of their oppressors, was written among the nations.

And this took place in the broad daylight of contemporary nationalities and national history. Egypt was then flourishing in the strength of her maturity under the Pharaohs. She was the oldest of the nations. Her monuments, which we ourselves have learnt to read within the last fifty years, go back for more than ten centuries before; and though they not unnaturally are silent upon this event, which was obviously attended with great national calamity, yet they so far establish the general accuracy of the Mosaic narrative that it is utterly impossible to call in question the main statements of it. There is a clear background of historical Egyptian nationality, on which is projected in strong and definite outline the first commencement of the independent existence of the Israelitish nation. And after all allowance is made for the partiality of the native historian, the material facts cannot have been very different from his narrative of them. Perhaps in all history there is no other instance but one which bears any strict analogy to the birth of Israel as a nation, and that was the memorable occasion when, on the 4th of July, 1776, the independence of the American Republic was declared in the Town Hall of Philadelphia. Then a nation was born at once, with the hope and promise of unlimited and unimaginable greatness. But with this exception there is, perhaps, no true parallel in the world's history to the definite and clearly marked manner in which the people of Israel entered on their existence as a nation. The date that is traditionally assigned to this event is about a thousand years before the battle of Marathon. At a period so remote we may well be uncertain as to exact time, and by some the date has been placed earlier, and by others later. The possible limit of variation is probably not much more than one hundred and fifty years either way; and however this is eventually decided, if decided it can ever be, the historic character of the event is independent and indisputable, and a national existence of many centuries is left for Israel before Greece or Rome began to appear upon the stage.

From the moment, however, that the national existence of Israel became a fact, the existence of the *race* became identified therewith, and marked thereby. No Israelite can sever himself from the past. His individual existence is stamped by the characteristics of his national history. He is, in spite of himself, a member of the nation that was born on the night of emancipation from Egypt, and there is no Israelite anywhere who can, if he would, disengage himself from the association of this connexion. It is different with the Mongol or the Negro. He belongs to a race but not to a nation. With Israel the race and the nation are one and the same.

Or take again the Gypsies, who may be thought to present some features analogous to those of the Jews. Strange as their habits are, they have scarcely the characteristics of a race, and certainly not those of a nation, for they have no national history, and therefore no national existence. But from the moment that Israel came out of Egypt to the present day, their national existence has been unbroken, and their national history continuous. That they have a continuous history is obvious, for it has many times been written, but they have also a continuous national existence, for they have a definite, individualised existence as a race which in every particular individual instance runs up into identity and community of historic national existence in the past. To no Israelite, in any quarter of the globe, can we assign a distinct historic nationality of less than three thousand years. For thirty centuries then, for a hundred generations, every Israelite throughout the world has had an individual existence, bequeathed from sire to son, and a share in a national existence, independent of the nations of the world. Captivity, conquest, oppression, violence, rapine, and cruelty, have alike been unable to obliterate these distinctions, and have served rather to make them yet more indelible. Words that were spoken in the early dawn of their national history have been strangely fulfilled to the last syllable of recorded time. "Lo, the people shall dwell alone, and shall not be reckoned among the nations."[1] In them and in them only the peculiarities of race have run up into and become identical with the peculiarities of national existence; and the great marvel has been that though not reckoned among the nations, the race of Israel have yet preserved distinct and uncontaminated their national existence.

And when we bear in mind the variety and vicissitude of circumstance under which this has been done, and the length of time that the national peculiarities have been maintained, it becomes a matter of certainty that there is no second instance to be produced altogether analogous. And the reason is that though similar peculiarities of race scarcely less permanent may possibly be found, there is no case in which there is added on to them the yet more striking phenomenon of identity of national existence. Wherever we find an Israelite, there we know we have a man whose ancestors were brought out of Egypt by Moses; but of no Greek can it be said that his ancestors fought at Marathon or Thermopylæ, and of no Roman that he is descended from the men who strove with Pyrrhus at Tarentum, or with Hannibal at Cannæ. All that in these cases can be said is, that the modern Greeks and Romans are apparently or possibly descended from the nations that originally were so distinguished.

[1] Num. xxiii. 9.

But in addition to the oneness of national existence that characterises the Jews wherever found there is another point in which they are pre-eminent, and that is in the antiquity of their national literature. This also is marked with the same features of unity and cohesion that distinguish their nation, and they are features that are peculiar to it. There is nothing in Greek or Roman literature at all answering to this unity and cohesion; except community of language, there is no principle of unity. There is nothing in common between Homer and Plato, between Cicero and Virgil, any more than there is between Bacon and Shakspeare. But there is a principle of unity and cohesion running through all the writers of the Old Testament. There is a strong principle of nationality. There is more or less a community of purpose, or object, and identity of teaching. It is not fortuitous that the Psalms, Isaiah, and Genesis are bound up together in the same volume, though the product of various ages and the work of various writers separated by an interval of a thousand years. They are intimately related, and we cannot but connect them. But no one would think of connecting together in the same way Sophocles and Plato, Virgil and Horace, though in these cases the fortuitous connexion of age and circumstance was far closer than between Moses, David, and Isaiah.

Nor is there anything answering to this essential unity in any other literature if we except the early

Christian literature, which grew out of and was based upon it. Take, for instance, the hymns of the Veda, the only literature which can pretend to compete with the old Hebrew literature in respect of antiquity. There is no principle of cohesion there. A family likeness runs through all, inasmuch as they are for the most part sacrificial and connected with the worship of Indra, Agni, Varuna, and the like. But there is no common nationality, no principle of inherent unity. They are no more essentially one than the songs of Horace or the odes of Pindar. But when we come to examine the Psalms, though the writers were separated by intervals of many centuries there is something more than an ideal unity pervading them. Many celebrate the same national incidents. All are addressed, more or less directly, to the same national God. All are instinct with the same conception of His nature, the same knowledge of His will, the same longing for or confidence in His favour. The Psalms are unique in the literature of the world, as the expression of the devotional spirit. More exclusively national than the hymns of the Veda, they yet speak the language of all the nations of the world; while the skill with which they have traversed and explored all the innermost recesses of the human heart is not only unsurpassed but altogether unequalled by any similar compositions, ancient or modern. They have knocked at the door of heaven and taken it by storm ; they have carried the soul on the wings of prayer to the very footstool of the throne of God ; and they have brought the Most High Himself from His holy habitation as a gracious visitant to the humble and contrite soul. If the Hebrew nation had produced nothing else but the Book of Psalms, it had laid all the families and generations of the world under a permanent obligation of insolvent gratitude.

But in point of fact this is but a fraction of the debt that is owing from mankind to the Hebrew race. That which confirmed the existence of the Israelitish nation after the exodus, and which moulded the national existence, and stamped upon it a character absolutely ineffaceable, was the *giving of the Law* from Sinai. We have heard of an English clergyman in recent years who renounced his orders because he could no longer find it in his conscience to repeat the formula, " God spake these words, and said, Thou shalt have none other gods but me: I am the Lord thy God, which brought thee out of the land of Egypt." But one would respectfully and with all due submission ask, Who else but God can have said " I am the Lord thy God"? Whose law is it but God's which says Thou shalt not kill, Thou shalt not commit adultery ? Is it a law which man has imposed upon himself ? Is it a law which the wisdom of the majority has discovered, and mankind have agreed in recognising ? Did Moses impose it upon Israel ? Did the people whom he characterised as stiff-necked and uncircumcised immediately submit to be imposed upon by him with out a doubt or question? Or were they, in spite of their stiffneckedness, at once and forthwith so enamoured of the wisdom and sublimity of his law that they without hesitation unanimously ascribed it, not to him, but to God, though they knew that he was really the author of it. There is and can be *no* question which all mankind are more concerned in than the question whether the moral law is Divine or human in its obligation; but if it is Divine in its *obligation* how is it possible that it can be other than Divine in its *origin*? And if it really is Divine in its origin, then I do not know that we can discover, and I am quite certain that history has not recorded, a more probable, consistent, congruous, or sublime theory of its origin than that which has been propounded and described as a fact by Moses.

But what must be the obligations of mankind to that people who were the first authoritative propounders of the moral law! Even supposing that we may have considerable difficulty in reducing the statements of Moses' narrative to the exact conditions of a narrative by a special correspondent of the *Times* or *Daily News*, we at all events have got as the nucleus of that narrative, after stripping it of all apparently supernatural accidents, the Decalogue itself, with its alleged Divine authority, preserved in letters as distinct and legible as those in which it was first written with the finger of God on the two tables of stone. And here is an heir-loom for the world. An absolutely complete and perfect moral law, the backbone and foundation of all laws which have ever regulated the conduct or controlled the actions of mankind; a law far more ancient than any which has been preserved among any people; far more simple, far more thorough, far more searching; a law the undoubtedly historical connexion of which with the name of Moses must alone and of itself give him a valid claim to be the very greatest benefactor of mankind that the ancient world ever saw, and must serve for all generations and for all time to place him, second only to One, as the greatest among all the great men that have ever lived. If the world consents to bestow its admiration upon the captains and conquerors who, from the very nature of their work, have been the destroyers of society, even though they may also have defended and avenged its interests, how shall we determine adequately to honour him, or acknowledge our immeasurable obligations to one who laid broad and deep the foundations of all human society by the first authoritative promulgation of the moral law, and thereby established his claim to be for ever regarded as the founder and preserver of society.

And it is not possible to separate the name of Moses from relation to the Decalogue. Even though we may acknowledge its origin to be never so much Divine, yet he, at all events, was the human agent by whom it was given to his people. He, therefore, humanly speaking, is entitled to the full credit of its wisdom. And whether we regard it as a Divine code, or prefer to judge it as a human law, the obligations of the world to its human author remain the same, for even supposing that he originated its actual form, he yet had the wisdom to see that its authority was Divine, and to propound it accordingly to the nation. And it was here that his law differed from all human codes, in that it was based upon man's relation to his Maker, and assumed the form of a direct covenant made between God and every individual of the nation. I am the Lord *thy* God : *thou* shalt have none other gods but me. The moral law thus became to every Israelite an essential part in the foundation of his nationality. Every violation of the moral law was to him an act of personal ingratitude towards the Being who had brought him and his fathers out of the land of Egypt. The foundation of the law was thus laid in that principle of love which was afterwards declared to be the *end* of the law.[1] And a line of demarcation was strongly and deeply drawn by the law between the children of Israel and all other nations of the earth.

Another characteristic which is peculiar to the literature of this remarkable people is the possession of unbroken historical records covering a period of

---

[1] Rom. x. 4.

nearly a thousand years, from the exodus till the return from captivity. It is in the highest degree improbable that this literature originated after the captivity. It bears all the appearance of being compiled from contemporary and authentic documents; but however this may be, there is no nation which has any literature at all to be compared to it. The Father of history did not begin to write till the historical records of Israel had come to an end. Opinions may vary as to the actual value of these records; the point to which I desire to draw attention is their existence, and their existence it is which distinguishes the literature of Israel from every other literature in the world. After the modern discoveries in Babylonia and the progress in decyphering the cuneiform inscriptions, comparisons will doubtless be instituted between the *brick* annals of Babylonia and Assyria, and those of Israel; but from the specimens as yet given to the world, we need not hesitate as to the result of those comparisons, while the very fact of such records having been discovered only serves to show conclusively that a neighbouring if not a kindred nation may well have preserved the annals of its history.

But there is yet another point in which this people and their literature are widely distinct from those of all other nations, and that is in the possession of prophecy and a race of prophets who committed their works to writing, which has preserved them to the present day. But prophecy is by no means peculiar to the so-called prophets of Israel or of Judah. Several very important prophecies are enshrined in Genesis, and in fact in every book of the Pentateuch. It is no part of my business now to insist upon the genuineness or antiquity of these prophecies. I am content to take my stand upon the very broadest possible ground. Let the Pentateuch in its present form have been written at the latest possible date on which the critics can agree, (we still reserve our own judgment on the matter),—there are yet prophecies, or at all events statements hazarded in those writings which cannot be placed late enough by them not to have been in existence ages before the occurrence of events which have made them strangely significant. Such, for instance, as the various promises made to Abraham, the blessing of the tribes of Jacob, and of Moses, the prophecies of Balaam, and those scattered over Deuteronomy, and in the twenty-sixth chapter of Leviticus. It is not too much to say that the entire literature of the world, in all languages combined, cannot present a series of apparent predictions so remarkable as those which are contained in the five books of Moses alone. And besides these there are predictions scattered over Joshua, Judges, the books of Samuel, Kings, and the Psalms, which may be safely said to defy adequate explanation if they are not prophecies, and which if they are can only be regarded as in the highest degree remarkable and important, before we enter upon the prophetical writings properly so called.

Written prophecy had an existence in the Hebrew nation of about 400 years. It is ascribed to fifteen different writers, or to sixteen including Daniel. They were all subsequent to the division of the monarchy, and did not exclusively belong to the kingdom of Judah. They were all alike characterised by the severely moral tone which they assumed. They were the censors of public morals, and the great preachers of the day. There is nothing in the literature of any ancient people at all corresponding to the phenomenon of prophecy as it existed in Israel and Judah. Indeed it is a phenomenon that would have been naturally impossible but for the peculiar position in which the nation stood to God, as testified by the Decalogue alone. No prophet could have spoken in the name of the Lord as he did had he not been taught by the previous history of his nation, and the salient points of its literature—as, for instance, the decalogue—the special and exceptional relation in which every member of the nation stood to God. In fact, all the writings of the prophets and their very existence may be said to be but one long commentary of fact and exhortation upon the ancient Mosaic words "I am the Lord thy God, which brought thee out of the land of Egypt and out of the house of bondage : thou shalt have none other gods before me."[1] But in thus speaking of the

[1] Exodus xx. 2, 3.

Hebrew Prophets it must not be forgotten that we are speaking of a race of men the very youngest of whom is more ancient than the whole of the Roman and the bulk of all the Grecian literature, and every one of the least of whom, judged by his own standard and on the written evidence before us, knew more of the relation in which he stood to God than Socrates did in his most inspired moments; and whose influence on the world at large has been far wider and deeper and more beneficial than that of Socrates. Take, for instance, the very last words of the least in bulk of the Hebrew Prophets, " And the kingdom shall be the Lord's."[1] Where, in all the writings of Xenophon, Plato, and Aristotle combined, is there any sentiment so far reaching, so permanent, so inexhaustible and so sure as that? And yet that perhaps was uttered nearly five-and-twenty centuries ago, before Socrates taught or Plato wrote; but it contains the germ and promise of all that they were feeling after and could not find. And it is either true or not true. If it is not true, then not only are the dreams of Plato more baseless than ever, but the destiny of man is a hopeless puzzle and his mere existence a disaster; but if it is true, then it is contrary to all analogy or experience that the insignificant Hebrew Prophet should have *discovered* its truth; nor, indeed, did he profess to have done so. In whatever sense it was true, and in pro-

[1] Obadiah 31.

portion as it was true, it must have been *revealed* to him. It must have come from God, and have been the word of the Lord, and it is true, and is only true, because the prophet was able to say in truth, without imposture or delusion, " Thus saith the Lord God." But this is nothing more nor less than what every prophet of Israel and of Judah said. They all alike professed to be the bearers of a Divine message, and to speak with authority not their own. And the verdict of many nations for little less than two thousand years has fully recognised and confirmed their claim.

But the most remarkable feature of the Hebrew prophets consisted in this, that they were ordained more than any men that ever lived as prophets to the world. Their message fell indeed upon their own nation, but it was of far wider scope. It was not only directed occasionally to the neighbouring nations, but it was given in trust to Israel for the world. The consciousness is not seldom bursting from the prophets that there is a mighty future in store for Israel. They knew that the covenant-God of Jacob would ultimately be acknowledged as the Lord of the whole earth. They promised that out of Zion should go forth the law, and the word of the Lord from Jerusalem ; that he should judge among the nations, and should rebuke many people. Nor is it a slender confirmation of their truth that in countries far distant, among alien races and languages of a different family, their message should have been accepted as the very word of God, and their honour should be as great as among the descendants of their own nation.

It was, however, not only visions of glory that the prophets saw for Israel; they declared in unmistakable language the then future destiny of the people, which marvellously corresponds to what it is at present. The great Lawgiver Himself had said, "And I will scatter you among the heathen, and will draw out a sword after you, and your land shall be desolate, and your cities waste"[1] and again, "And the Lord shall scatter thee among all people, from the one end of the earth even to the other;"[2] and Nehemiah, living under the close of the Old Testament times, had acknowledged the truth of that promise; and Haman had said to King Ahasuerus, "There is a certain people scattered abroad and dispersed among the people in all the provinces of thy kingdom, and their laws are diverse among all people."[3] But in neither case had the words of Moses received the illustration that the history of the last eighteen centuries has given them. The dispersion must now be tenfold more than it was then, or for ages afterwards, and it is now and has been for years the great and unique ethnological problem for which we cannot naturally account. But the Hebrew prophets have accounted for it, for Amos wrote twenty-five centuries

[1] Lev. xxi. 33. [2] Deut. xxviii. 64. [3] Esther iii. 8.

ago, "For lo, I will command, and I will sift the house of Israel among all nations, like as corn is sifted in a sieve; yet shall not the least grain fall upon the earth."[1] The scattering therefore of the Hebrew nation was a fact foreseen in the providence of God; upon the written evidence of their own prophets, which we have seen, there is so much ground for treating with the utmost deference. But it is only one feature. Notwithstanding the national attachment to the law, the national observance of the law is and has been for eighteen centuries a thing impossible; and this also the prophets had declared, for Hosea had said, "The children of Israel shall abide many days without a king, and without a prince, and without a sacrifice, and without an image, and without an ephod, and without teraphim; afterwards shall the children of Israel return and seek the Lord their God and David their king, and shall fear the Lord and His goodness in the latter days."[1] Part of this has long been fulfilled to the very letter, and part of it yet awaits fulfilment. For centuries the Jews have had neither king nor prince nor sacrifice. For centuries it has been impossible for them to keep the annual feasts according to the prescriptions of the law. While, therefore, the Jewish nation is bound by ties that cannot be severed to their law, their history, and their prophets, which alone give any explanation of the actual phenomena of their

[1] Amos ix. 9. [2] Hosea iii. 4, 5.

past and present existence, they are nevertheless unable to comply with the requirements of the law to which they owe their nationality, although the injunction with which prophecy expired was, "Remember ye the law of Moses my servant, which I commanded unto him in Horeb, for all Israel, with the statutes and judgments;"[1] and though the Lawgiver himself gave utterance to the solemn warning, "Cursed be he that confirmeth not the words of this law to do them."[2]

But, furthermore, the law, the history, the Psalms, and the Prophets of Israel alike bear witness to an inextinguishable hope on the part of the Jewish nation, of the rise of a great Personage who should be the flower and glory of their race. No critical interpretation of the records can do away with the actual ground for this hope, because its existence for the first thousand years of the Christian era is one of the patent and unquestionable facts of history witnessed by the testimony of their own greatest writers. While, therefore, their national existence and their national history testify to the validity and truth of their ancient prophecies, they are constrained to confess that those prophecies have failed in the most characteristic and significant particular of the national hope of the Messiah. The national portraiture of Israel has been sketched by an unerring hand, but the portrait of the Messiah,

---

[1] Mal. iv. 4.   [2] Deut. xxvii. 26.

which is yet more Divine and masterly, has been a misconception and a failure, not because history has not supplied a counterpart to the prophetic delineation, but because the national face has been persistently averted from the counterpart that has been supplied. Israel, as a nation, is obliged to confess that for many centuries, both before and after Christ, the hope of a Messiah was its glory and joy. Israel as a nation is obliged to confess that there is no one in all history that has vindicated and realised the hope of the nation, if Jesus of Nazareth is not he; and yet Israel, as a nation, is obliged also to confess as a historic fact that it is through the preaching of the first disciples of Jesus of Nazareth, and through them alone, that the fairest and most enlightened kingdoms of the civilised world have been led to acknowledge the God of Israel as their own God, and to acknowledge none other gods but Him. The relation of Israel, therefore, to their own Scriptures is one of the most inexplicable problems of literature and of history; nor does it seem possible to solve it but by the introduction of a third element, which is that of the rise of the Christian Church and the existence of the Christian literature, and that does completely and effectually solve it, for it shows that the promised ingathering of the nations has been made, not to Moses, or David, or Isaiah, as kings and prophets in themselves, but to the Prophet greater than Moses, even to Jesus, the Son of

David, by the proclamation of Him as the Christ of God, "the end of the law for righteousness to every one that believeth . . . to the Jew first and also to the Gentile."[1]

[1] Rom. x. 4; i. 16.

IV.

The Relation of the Jews to the Nations at Large.

BY

THE RIGHT REV. BISHOP CLAUGHTON, D.D.

IV.

THE RELATION OF THE JEWS TO THE NATIONS AT LARGE.

IT is an objection not unfrequently made to the revealed history of creation, that there has been a failure in what is set before us as God's own design, and especially in what we must believe to have been His chief object, *mankind.* The entering in of evil into the world, which had been pronounced "very good;" the startling expression, "It *repented* God that He had made man on the earth" (Gen. vi. 6)—these are adduced as an evident admission of failure, in itself incompatible with the entire theory of absolute goodness and almighty power.

It does not seem to occur to such reasoners that Scripture itself puts it into their power to adduce these objections, or that there must be some very obvious reason for an admission which might seem to contradict God's own declaration,—nay, the very letter of the assertion—"the gifts and calling of God are without repentance," (Rom. xi. 29)—shews clearly that there is some very simple reconciliation of the apparent incongruity. It is, indeed, not uncommon for revelation to employ the form of speech which we call "paradox;" and it is one, we may safely assert, of which the great value is that it intensifies the truth which it asserts. More than this, it is often a correct description of the mode in which God works His ends. Thus evil is permitted to enter and to mar the world He had made. Sin comes into it, and death by sin; but redemption takes away sin, and resurrection destroys death. And the very fact of having sin to conquer is a means of attaining holiness and virtue; whilst a world redeemed is but added and greater glory to the Creator. "*An enemy hath done this.*" Here is the *admission*, but as the parable goes on—the very illustration of the world's history in its brief sentence—we see the final triumph of good over evil—" In the time of harvest I will say," etc. Matt. xiii. 30).

This view is most strikingly illustrated in the Mosaic account of the separation of the various races of mankind. The first great judgment after the fall had come, the very face of the earth had been changed,—a change to which its surface still bears witness,—but men, beginning to recover their lost numbers, and fresh from the dread of the punishment which had fallen upon them, devised the strange scheme of defence by union against God. This He made impossible by the confusion of tongues, and sent them forth as *nations*, working out His own gracious design of good, whilst chastening them, and preparing them for another and better ultimate unity than any they could have devised, bringing them to be again one *family*, when they had first learned to acknowledge His goodness, and been taught by the experience of His judgments to submit themselves to His power.

It is to this period of the history of mankind that I would draw your attention to-day, and to the feature in God's design which I have noticed in my opening remarks, viz., how He makes very *opposites* combine in working His will. From the scattering of the various families of the earth into nations we date the commencement of the building up of the unity of mankind as one family; at first, as it might seem, only by a wide separation, the choosing of one family, to be for long years kept distinct and marked off from the rest, for the preservation of the one principle on which only true unity could rest, —the worship and acknowledgment of *the One God*.

It is this principle which marks the choosing of one family or race from amongst the rest. Abraham appears as God's servant, a believer in His love and goodness, maintaining the ordinances that we have most clearly noticed in Scripture—that, for instance, of sacrifice—and carefully bringing up his family to the same right belief,—selected, indeed, to be the recipient of special promises and signs from God Himself, and in his whole life a pattern of devotion and obedience. The part assigned to him seems to be the natural reward of his own character. He is the *father* of the faithful, the '*believer*' of his generation, as his ancestor Noah had been at a yet earlier date. We pass over the record of his immediate successors? We find a nation emerging from Egypt, under the guidance of Moses, whose history very soon places them in a prominence such as no other nation ever has attained. It is not their *power* or their warlike strength, their wealth or their territorial empire, that distinguishes them,—they are God's own people. His hand is visibly extended to protect and guide them. They have, we may say in few words, a history such as no other race can pretend to claim. Miracles follow their footsteps,—their very sins are punished as no other nation's sins are punished. They lived under a system of immediate rewards and punishments. God is their actual Sovereign, and when in their folly they choose a king to reign over them his selection is by the voice of their Almighty Ruler, as the *Judges* of a yet earlier period had been simply persons raised up to execute His will. I need not follow their history in its details. It is familiar to us, and before us all.

We call to mind the wonders of the wilderness and the entry into the promised land; we see in our mind's eye the glorious Temple rise at Jerusalem; we picture the greatness of Solomon,—a greatness which cast its shadow over the whole East. It matters not, indeed, which period or portion of this remarkable race's fortunes we observe. With themselves we remember the wonders of their old time,— what their fathers have told us,—"God hath not dealt so with any nation;" with them we say, "The Lord hath chosen Jacob unto Himself, and Israel for His own possession." Their creed evidently holds in itself that of mankind; their Scriptures are the evidence of its truth, and in their hands is, in God's providence, the destiny of the human race. Such, and not less than this, is the position of the great Jewish nation of whom I am to speak to you to-day. None of you can say I derogate from their greatness in what I have advanced; and yet I have said nothing but what every Christian in effect believes. What, I now ask, is the legitimate conclusion of such high claims? What must we look for at the hands of a race with such credentials as these? If I were speaking of Christianity, I might show you that all this great past was to lead to a great future, that the real source of the greatness of Abraham's race was that in his seed " all the families of the earth were to blessed"; but I am going to confine my remarks to a narrower circle of questions, nay, to one single question—What is the relation in which this nation stands with regard to the other nations?—how do they discharge, if they do discharge, the functions of the high office they hold as God's witnesses to mankind? It needs not much reasoning to prove that the duty of Jews to the other races of the earth is singularly clear and plain. I do not think they were meant to be their actual teachers; they were to preserve the great truths of Revelation for later times, and, whether they accept it or no, they have been the instruments of such a preservation of revealed truth for ourselves, who have "entered" (in this sense) into their labours. We use their Scriptures, the words of their Prophets, the types and forms of their religious worship, in *establishing* the correctness of our own faith.

I want, however, to press this much further. I want to ask, What effect are they producing— nay, what effect have they in all these long years produced upon *other races?* Are those races, bettered by their sojourn amongst them? Is their religion, not only by its own evidence, but by the example of themselves its professors making way amongst the religions of the world? You may say, "Such was not the task imposed upon them; they were to maintain (as they have done) their belief against opposition,—to hand down (as they also have done) the same belief to their children." I utterly deny that this is all or the chief part of what is laid upon them; they are to teach others, at least by example, and, putting religion aside, they are to regenerate the nations of the earth with the effect of their own high privilege—the knowledge of the true and only God. Have they done so in any perceptible degree ? Can they maintain with any show of reason that their position amongst the nations of the earth is that of a race which has blessed those amongst whom they sojourned, and whose history if they passed away (as races have passed away as to any distinct existence) would be that of a people who spread civilization and taught a higher morality in all the lands where they dwelt? I must say it plainly—the reverse is the fact; they have received rather than conferred benefit; their own moral and social position has been improved by dwelling amidst those whose laws had already been improved, whose social system had been elevated,— I do not mean to say necessarily by Christianity as the direct cause, but by all the various accompaniments and effects of Christianity; and I add that the Jews have rather sought these races than others their inferiors in these important respects. We do not find them dwelling amongst the ignorant and degraded Africans or the Hindoos, but amongst the Christians of Europe,—the Mohammedan in a less degree ; and whilst from the latter they seem to have gained nothing and imparted nothing to them, from the former they have obtained education (and, to their credit, valued and used it). The laws governing their social condition have been improved. I do not say this as depreciating them in comparison with other nations ; but I must contend that in a degree this fact it derogates from any claim of superiority they may make in their present condition.

I should here carefully distinguish what I am saying from any depreciation of the high character of individuals of the race I am thus canvassing so freely, or, indeed, of the entire people. We know them as dwellers in our midst, we respect their many virtues as good citizens, we know that in any good work of beneficence they set us an example; and I should be doing injustice to my own feelings if I did not give expression both to my own high esteem for them and to the deep interest I feel both in their character and in their fortunes. I look on them as destined to occupy a position even in relation to our own Christianity of no common importance. What I lament is that they do not, so far as we can judge, take the same view of *themselves*. It is not enough that they should be men of mark amongst us for wealth, for charity, for aid towards objects of high education and political benefit to us all. I have worked at their side in some of the various matters of the day; I have met them in social converse and friendship; it is in their place that I am, as it were, putting myself, when I urge upon them not to subside into a mere monument of a great past, but to prove their high ancestry by a course worthy of and corresponding to the deeds of their fathers and the words of their prophets. Almost every nation has a past; the origin of a people is usually the portion of its history that lives, or more frequently perhaps, the point where it culminates and reaches its climax. But the history of Israel is not great only, but its promised future is more glorious than anything that has gone before. For them, to live in the past is itself a decadence and a fall. We, whose own faith is bound up in theirs, have a right to speak to them in this strain. We who have stood on the shores of the Red Sea, where even now those who tread its soil, though of a different faith, believe the record; we who are applying their Psalms and prophecies to our own souls, and our own lives,—we may well claim to say to them of their own Zion, "We 'think upon her stones ; it pitieth us to see her in the dust'" (Psalm cii.).

I ask, then, is the true relation of this remarkable race to the rest of the nations simply what history and our own experience tell us it has been? Some special object and use in the world, it must be believed, was assigned to them : are they discharging it, fulfilling their high destiny? Take their case as compared with Mohammedans, the latter, with an erroneous creed, only true so far as it is in accordance with the Jewish Scriptures and our own, have evidently no special use except so far as God has turned their very crimes into His own instruments of good. I do not ignore the exceptional appearance of a sort of missionary spirit amongst Mohammedans in some parts of the world, and I do not sympathise with the harsh expressions that, in the late controversy, some have used regarding them. I only assert that it would be a wild and untenable theory to maintain that we were to look to the Mohammedans for the amelioration of our race; it is clear that we must reverse the position: it is our task to raise and improve them,—not by the sword, but by our influence and example, and, I am bold to add, (waiting for the opportunity and the call) by direct teaching of the truths we hold. Compare, however, the position of Jews with that of Mohammedans. Ought these not, to be a very *contrast* with the latter? Are they not—putting out of the question political relations—simply in a like position, teaching nothing,—*forgetting nothing*, we may almost add? What great principles of glorious hope for man, what high enthusiasm for the deliverance of God's noblest creature from the thraldom of his own errors or passions, have emanated from one or the other of these remarkable families of mankind! Yet do not let me be supposed for a moment to place them on an equality: for the one there is present empire, threatened, no doubt, with peril which may prove its ruin; for the other, I ask, is there not a field and a future greater than that of empire,—their gathering together, as one people, to Jerusalem, itself? It is not, indeed, that I speak of, though I do not hold it either impossible or unlikely; indeed, in some sense, this will take place in God's own time and God's own way, but "His ways are not our ways," and it is by events often that we discover His plan. We have to obey His word and trust His promise, and He "will bring it to pass."

Faith, however, implies action. The time is long past for His once chosen people simply to maintain a worship and a creed; doubtless that worship preserved the creed in dark and troublous times. The hour of action has arrived, and a choice must be made. We Christians are moving according to the command given to us, to "go and teach all nations." We may often fail, we have sometimes fearfully neglected the work, but by God's mercy it is still in our hands to do. We are the teachers of the nations. To you we turn, men of Israel, through whom we received our credentials, and say, Take part with us in our ministry; too long have ye waited inactive. "The kingdom of God cometh not with *observation*." Join us and restore the glories of your own past, or rather, see them merged and lost in the greater triumphs of the Heir of David, your own and our Messiah, the Shiloh to whom the gathering of the nations shall be (Gen. xlix. 10). "O Jerusalem, Jerusalem," cried He who *loved* it with more than human love, "how often would I have gathered thy children together"

(Luke xiii. 34); but in His very words there was a latent promise, a condition offered, of late but effectual repentance. "Your house is left unto you desolate." The words are true to the letter, fulfilled before your eyes. Is not the promise equally so which foretells the end of desolation and the day of glad belief at last? "Ye shall not see this until the time come when ye shall say, Blessed is He that cometh in the name of the Lord."

There remains one question yet more clearly affecting the sons of Judah—their relation to their own brethren, the tribes of Israel, separated for a time in the mysterious counsels of God, but this separation one that clearly cannot be accepted as final by themselves. The sad disruption that followed on the cry of offended Israel, "What portion have we in David? now see to thine own house, David" (1 Kings xii. 16), has surely in these long years had its answer,—not such as they fashioned in their own blind anger. They have simply, as far as their own act tended, blotted themselves out of history; but *not so*. The true tenor of all the great promises to Abraham and his seed utterly forbids such an interpretation of God's designs. Special promises, doubtless, attach to Judah; but almost every scripture that speaks of them adds the glory of Ephraim as part of the mighty future of the chosen race. If the Patriarch whose name yet marks the royal tribe, saved Joseph the future preserver of all his brethren, it was the common fortune of all that were in his hand. And Christian writers never failed to see this. "To the *twelve tribes* which are *scattered abroad*, greeting," is the heading of the Epistle of *St. James*; by birth a Jew, by faith the first Christian Bishop at Jerusalem. Nay, yet higher authority remains. The Book of Revelation, which foretells the "things that must be hereafter," omits (save one) no tribe in the list of those enumerated as amongst the 'sealed' for acceptance in the last great day (Rev. vii.). That awful omission has a parallel in the record of God's dealings with His once called disciples —one afterwards unhappily found faithless. And as He that "judged His people as one of the tribes of Israel," became a serpent by the way, an adder in the path (Gen. xlix. 16, 17), so Iscariot, the son of Simon, "was guide to them that took Jesus" (Acts i. 16), and his name is not found after the brief record of his sin and its punishment, and "another took his office." If I introduce mention of this history, it is for the happier contrast in the hope I would have all (especially *themselves*), entertain who care to read the wondrous annals of this peculiar race of a great and noble future that is before them,—not their own glory alone or chiefly, but a great debt they owe to mankind, and, as I now remind them, to their own brethren lying hid for the present and lost amongst the nations—missing as they are said to be to our eyes, but not to *Him*

Who is the Redeemer of Israel, Who "saith to the prisoners, Go forth ; to them that are in darkness, Show yourselves" (Isa. xlix.).

I have not made it my object in these remarks to urge upon the sons of Judah the great debt they owe to Christianity, which has ever clung to belief in their high destiny, and (however its own history may be disfigured by some traits of cruel injustice and persecution in dark superstitious days) cherished as a part of its own creed a recognition of the great part they have yet to play in the regenerating of the nations. I ask them the more confidently to listen to the plea that I urge—that they should view soberly and honestly the relation in which they stand to mankind at large. Have they not been singled out in God's providence in the past? Are they not now fulfilling a wonderful and unexampled destiny—scattered in every land, dwelling amongst the nations,—having a part, yet no part, in their polity and their fortunes?

What, I ask, then, must the end be? "Search the Scriptures," said One to them of old, "for in them ye think ye have eternal life;" and still to their own Scripture we refer them,—"to the law and to the testimony" (Isa. viii. 20). And there we read, "There shall be a root of Jesse, which shall stand for an ensign of the people ; to it shall the Gentiles seek" (Isa. xi. 10-13). "And it shall come to pass in the day that the Lord shall set His hand the second time to recover the remnant of His people. . . . And He shall set up an ensign for the nations, and shall assemble the outcasts of Israel. . . . " For the Lord will have mercy on Jacob, and will yet choose Israel, and set them in their own land : (Is. xiv. 1) and the strangers shall be joined with them."

V.

On the Comparative Effects of Judaism and Christianity upon the World.

BY

THE REV. DONALD FRASER, D.D.

V.

ON THE COMPARATIVE EFFECTS OF JUDAISM AND CHRISTIANITY UPON THE WORLD.

THE topic assigned to us does not lead into disputed interpretation of ancient oracles, or a discussion of the origin and *rationale* of religious belief; what is proposed is to apply to the religious systems known as Judaism and Christianity the practical test of usefulness to mankind. Let us compare them as respects the power to bless the world at large which each of them has shown in the course of history.

When, however, we apply such a test to religion —any religion—we must keep certain conditions and explanations in view; *e.g.* (1.) We do not seize on this as a primary and fundamental test of truth. Enough that proved usefulness supplies a presumption in support of a religious system before its truth has been otherwise investigated, and a corroboration of the verdict when an investigation has issued favourably; for all who believe in God and in His beneficent government of the world, must admit that a true religion, pleasing to Him, must be expected to have a loving aspect towards mankind, and to produce good and happy results wherever its influence extends. (2.) When we speak of utility we do not mean popularity, or the adherence of vast numbers to a religious banner, for truth is not determined by majorities. We mean well-approved adaptation to the moral and spiritual wants of many nations, and the production of holy and beneficial effects upon the world. (3.) The test must be applied on a large scale of history and observation, if it is to be of any real use. The view must range over many countries and many generations. Concomitant and incidental effects must be distinguished from essential and invariable fruits. For attendant evils allowance must be made according to the best information within our reach, that we may arrive at the *nett* practical result, and put that, and that only, to the credit of a religion in our comparative estimates.

No son of Abraham can forbid us to apply such a test to his religion.[*] Let it be that the law given

---

[*] The "Jewish World," in a critical notice of this lecture, abandons all claim to propagate Judaism, and denounces the propagation of Christianity as "an impracticable task, and an unmitigated curse." "The especial mould in which our religion is cast is determined by race. We claim Judaism for the Jews. It is not our province to dictate what special form the religions of other people shall assume. . . . It is by the development, not of any particular system, but of the parent interests of Humanity that the world is to be really elevated."— *Jewish World*, 11th May, 1877.

And to this poor rationalistic level have fallen some of the children of Abraham!

under Moses, which moulded Israel into a nation, separated them to Jehovah from all the world around, and that the effect of their theocratic institutions was to place them in a position of sharp contrast to the neighbouring peoples and tribes; still there is a larger and kindlier aspect of Abraham's tent, and of David's throne.

Abraham was chosen, called, and placed in covenant relation to God for this very end—that in his posterity all families of the earth might be blessed. It will not be alleged that this blessing was designed to consist of secular benefits, as that the descendants of that patriarch were to teach arts and sciences to other nations, to be the first discoverers, builders, or engineers. Indisputably, the promise meant that by their faith, or in their religious character, Abraham's posterity would be of the highest service to mankind. And no one who glories in having Abraham for a father can complain if the religion he professes be brought to this test: Has it blessed, and is it now blessing the families, or tribes, and nations of the earth?

The same observation applies to David's throne. Its glory was to appear in its beneficent aspect to the world. A great Hebrew song of the Davidic royalty has these words: "Let men bless themselves in Him; let all nations call Him blessed." No one will say that such language bears on the mere political welfare of mankind, and that the royal sway of the Son of David over the world is meant to be just of the same nature with that of the Ptolemies or the Cæsars. It is a sacred and religious value that David's throne has for all the earth. And no Israelite or Jew who believes in his own sacred poetry, as having a genuine prophetic strain, can complain of the question, Who is the king? Where is that Son of David who blesses all nations, and whose name all nations reverence?

A Christian can just as little as a Jew refuse the test which we propose to apply. He professes to have a religion founded on the Hebrew basis. He affirms that the Christ in whom He believes is by emphasis "the seed of Abraham," and "the Son of David." Therefore he is bound to show that the promises made to the lineage of Abraham and the throne of David are being fulfilled by or through Jesus whom he affirms to be Christ. Nay, more; he is bound to this by the primary conception of Christianity. Though Jesus Christ did not Himself go to the Gentiles, He proclaimed the love of God to the world, and sent out His apostles with good tidings to all nations. There was some hesitation and delay before those Apostles quite understood the extent of their commission; but it is historically certain that they, and the other missionaries whom they associated with them, did preach the gospel as addressed and applicable to the world at large. There is therefore no alternative for a Christian but to submit the religion which he professes to this test: Has it, or has it not, on the whole blessed and bettered the nations of the earth? Has it approved itself as adapted to the moral and spiritual wants of mankind at large?

Both parties, then, in the great controversy with which this course of lectures deals, are obliged to admit the application of this very practical test. We proceed to apply it; and as we do so, endeavouring to review with all candour " the comparative effects of Judaism and Christianity upon the world," we must keep in mind that the distinction between these systems is not like that which subsists between two modes of faith radically different and unconnected, as between Christianity and Buddhism or Parseeism. By Judaism, in this discussion, we must mean anti-Christian Judaism, for only this can form a contrast to Christianity; and it is a very important element in the whole case, that the two systems of which we treat are not radically different, but radically connected. Rightly or wrongly, the Church was born out of the Temple and the Synagogue. And Christianity, equally with that Judaism to which it is now opposed, claims to have at its back the old Hebrew faith, and the venerable Scriptures in which that faith is enshrined.

First then, let us survey the relation borne to the world by that pre-Christian Judaism, or rather Hebrewism, about which we have no controversy

It was a witness for the unity of God, and for His law of righteousness maintained for centuries by one chosen nation, when all the world lay in darkness and the shadow of death. That elect nation was not always faithful to this calling, or true to this testimony; but even an imperfect loyalty to such a religion placed the tribes of Israel in well-defined opposition to the surrounding world. Their rites and ceremonies were their own; and their religious temper was exclusive. The Hebrews regarded the nations, the *Goyim*, as a profane mass, which they might have to fight, but with which they could not mingle. Their thought was not of converting the nations, but of subduing them in the name of Jehovah.

And yet, in the Old Testament the spirit of prophecy had larger thoughts, and cast a more gracious light upon the Gentiles. The bards of Israel in the Psalter have strains of great severity toward the nations, but also strains of benevolence and hope. They stigmatize the Gentiles as idolaters who deserve to be smitten with the sword, and humiliated before the theocratic king. They compose patriotic songs to celebrate victory, and to incite the people of Jehovah to do valiantly in future conflicts with the heathen. But kinder thoughts also breathe through these Psalms, recalling the old promise of the Abrahamic epoch about the blessing of all families of the earth. The stern exclusive spirit cries, " The nations compassed me about; but in the name of Jehovah I will destroy them." The more benevolent temper or wider sympathy of the old religion has expression in the words, " O praise Jehovah, all ye nations; celebrate Him, all ye peoples." "Let all the earth be filled with His glory."

The same double strain is plainly found in the great prophets of Judah. Isaiah and Jeremiah foretell heavy judgments incurred by the proud and idolatrous nations of the East ; but they also predict a return of nations to the service of Jehovah, or a reconciliation of the world to God; and, beyond the dark days of conflict and carnage, reveal a golden age of righteousness and peace. In their eyes Mount Zion is a hill of blessing for all the earth ; and the ultimate joy of Jerusalem is to be the centre of the joy of all mankind.

Not only had the religious books of the Hebrews (which are reverenced by modern Jews and Christians alike) this aspect of mingled severity and goodness toward the world at large, but the Hebrew people exhibited more or less distinctly in their history a corresponding twofold relation to the tribes and nations around them. During their times of fidelity to Jehovah they were separate from the heathen, witnesses against their idolatry and licentiousness; yet they received strangers into the commonwealth of Israel, and even when there was no such ingathering they did something in their dispersion to diffuse among other races a knowledge of the supreme Jehovah, and the hope of a future reign of justice and of truth. At one time or other, this people, numerically small, but influential from their very singularity, touched all the great nations and systems of antiquity, and were a blessing in the midst of all countries wherein they were scattered. Thus, in a measure, though in quite a limited measure, the families of the earth got a blessing through the seed of Abraham.

But a very remarkable fact now strikes our view. As the Roman power overspread the known world, the Jews settled in large numbers in Gentile cities, enjoying, on the whole, under the Roman prætors protection and security. They lived and worshipped apart, receiving from the authorities a half-contemptuous toleration; and they were content with this. Some of the heathen, for one cause or another, resorted to their synagogues as proselytes; but the Jews made no attempt to enlighten and bless the world. Their ancestral belief had come to be burdened with minute Rabbinical traditions, and any fervour that remained showed itself in a narrow fanaticism. So they had not faith enough to attempt the overthrow of heathen religions; and they had not love enough to become channels of blessing to the Gentiles. Judaism was more than ever before in contact with Gentilism; but there appeared in it no power, hardly any disposition, to bless the nations. It was becoming more and more formal, traditional, pedantic, fanatical, self-righteous, and self-enclosed.

Now mark what ensued. At that very time there arose at an obscure village in Galilee, one Jesus. He grew up under the veil of obscurity, reared among mechanics, trained in no Rabbinical school, and, so far as appears, not cast into association with cultured intellects. This Man, after He became known to His countrymen, had only a short career of perhaps three years; and during that time, though He attracted a few followers, and sometimes even crowds, He was steadily opposed by the leaders of the Jewish people, and at their instance was put to a shameful death. He did not visit other lands, or express any wish to confer with learned men, or so much as to see the chief seats of human knowledge and power. But this Jesus somehow began to exert an influence upon the world, learned and unlearned, greater than the most famous prophets of Israel had ever done. While displaying a knowledge of the ancient Scriptures which surprised the Jews, and showing the highest honour for "the law and the prophets," He gave to His teaching a breadth and fulness quite unknown to the contemporary teachers of His nation, but in harmony with the larger and brighter thoughts of the ancient prophets. He dealt with matters great in themselves, and supremely important to all men. He declared the Father whom the world had not known. He announced the kingdom of God. He proclaimed Himself in Jerusalem to be the Light of the world. And having trained certain disciples, and infused His own spirit into them, He bade them make more disciples in all the nations.

Those messengers whom he sent forth were themselves men of Israel—men of Galilee. They had the narrow ideas of their time and nation, and found it hard to believe that Gentiles should be placed on a par with the seed of Abraham. But, obeying the command of their Master, they lifted up their testimony to the Jew first, then to the Samaritan, and then to the Gentile; and lo! they began to act upon the world with a power that had never shown itself in even the most eminent men of the Hebrew race. Abraham, Joseph, Moses, Solomon, Daniel—all these played a great part with reference to the Gentiles in their time. But the fishermen of Galilee, and Paul of Tarsus, and Apollos of Alexandria, with others of the same stamp, turned the world upside down. They resisted the churlish separatism into which Judaism had degenerated; and they did what the most religious Jews throughout the Roman Empire had shrunk from attempting —they combated heathenism in its strongholds, and assailed it with success.

These began to be called Christians, and between them and the bulk of their own nation a great gulf opened. Though they took Jewish grounds of argument and belief, and dwelt on the promises made to the Hebrew fathers, they were dealt with as renegades, and the heathen were incited by the Jews to treat them with violence. Nevertheless, their testimony prevailed. The movement which began with those plain men of Galilee, who affirmed that Jesus was the Christ and the Son of the living God, could not be stayed by emperors or prætors, by priests or rabbis, by philosophers or satirists, by magistrates or mobs.

But now we are come to the parting of the roads, or of the streams. Judaism pursues one way, Christianity another. Judaism flows in one channel, Christianity in another. The former is in a narrow bed, hemmed in by Talmudic commentary and the traditions of the elders, flowing continuously through the world, but holding itself apart. The latter flows in a wide, strong stream, sometimes turbid enough, it must be confessed, but full of diffusive life, and touching in its course all human interests,—the domestic circle, morals, education, liberty or slavery, public spirit, and every part of the social economy; and that, too, in every nation which has received the Christian faith. Surely it is a fair question: In which of these ways or channels is the promise being fulfilled, that all families of the earth should be blessed? Both come from Abraham; for, as we have already pointed out, Christianity looks back as reverentially as Judaism to the father of the faithful, and in point of fact has done far more than modern Judaism to make known to the world Abraham and the Patriarchs, Moses and the Prophets. We think it clear, and mean to maintain, that the modern or anti-Christian Judaism has had a very feeble, if any, world-blessing influence; and that it is Christianity—notwithstanding the corruptions and superstitions that have infected and weakened it—that has shown a real power to bless the families of the earth.

Let us consider the great truth of monotheism, of which the Jews have unquestionably been the witnesses. Even in the former "times of ignorance," the pre-Christian centuries, we cannot see that the Jews have any ground to boast of the way in which they fiulfilled their high commission; for it appears from their own Scriptures that they were continually hankering after the gods of the heathen round about; and, in fact, never were for any long time steadfast monotheists till after their return from captivity in Babylon. But the question before us has reference to post-Christian and anti-Christian Judaism, and we ask what effect it has given to its testimony; what has it done during the past eighteen centuries to convince the world that there is but one living and true God? We do not forget or deny that the Jews occasionally suffered under the Roman Emperors for their absolute refusal to acknowledge the gods of their heathen rulers. This for their own consistency. But what did they then, and what have they done since that time to spread monotheism through the world? After Christianity arose, the Jews seem to have lost the power of making proselytes which they had before, and it became a rare thing for Gentile converts to appear in the synagogue. As for the great overthrow of heathenism, no one can ascribe it to the Jews. They were not the men that smote with withering force the vast polytheism of the ancient world. They were not the men who brought Europe and the north of Africa and Western Asia to cast away their idols. What they cared for was that they themselves should be better than others, and that Jehovah should delight in them. They did not love the world, and took no trouble, ran no risk, displayed no zeal to bring the nations to Jehovah's feet. Mohammedanism, in fact, has done far more to spread monotheism over a large part of the globe than Judaism. And Christianity has done immeasurably more. It has thrown down the shrines and images of false gods all over the earth. It does so still with undiminished zeal. And whereas the world, for all that Judaism does, might continue as polytheistic and idolatrous as it was two thousand years ago, Christianity is busy now in exposing and abolishing the heathenism of India, of China, of Central and Southern Africa, and of the Islands in the Pacific; just as in former days it destroyed the Druidical native worship of the

Gauls and Britons, and drove away the legendary gods of Germany and the North; or, in days still more remote, put an end to the worship of Isis and Serapis, of Jupiter and Apollo, and Venus, and Bacchus, and Pan.

It is notorious that the Jews avoid those countries where their monotheistic testimony is most needed. In heathen communities they are hardly ever seen. It is among Christians they live, where their witness to one God is not required, or among Mohammedans, with whom they have much sympathy; for they have these things in common: They say that there is one God—Jehovah—Allah. They boast of a great prophet—Moses—Mohammed. They have everything in a book—the Torah—the Koran. Withal they are self-righteous, and despise others.

But let us enquire whether, in other ways, modern Judaism has conferred blessings on the world. What of moral culture and attainment? The Jew boasts of that law, which (as Mordecai says to Daniel Deronda) " has carried within its frame the breath of social justice, of charity, and of household sanctities." But is it the Jew who has taught these virtues to the nations? Who has spread over the earth the Ten Commandments? Is it not the Christian? And who has driven into the conscience of the human race a great sentiment of duty which may be violated but cannot be crushed? Is it the Jew? Who can deny that it is the Christian, the man under law to Christ, who has received the ethics of the old legislation as expounded in the teaching of Jesus Christ, enforced by His authority, and written on fleshy tables of the heart by the power of His Holy Spirit? We do not for a moment dispute that high specimens of moral integrity have been and are exhibited among the Jews. What we point out is that not the Christ-rejecting Jews, but those, whether Jews or Gentiles, who have followed Christ, have made much moral impression on the world.

It is too true that the impression has been imperfect, and that much remains to be done in the moral education of mankind; but in so far as men of many nations have learned the baseness of deceit and selfishness, and the beauty and obligation of justice, truth, and love, the lesson has been received from that Christianity which has all along its history been, though with varying efficiency, according to its purity at different periods, the great aggressive instrument of moral civilization. This is all the more remarkable, because Christianity has often been represented in such a way as to do it great injustice. Unrighteous and cruel deeds have been perpetrated, and gross frauds have been practised in its dishonoured name; yet it has had vigour enough to survive and correct those evils, and to impress on mankind great ideas and motives of equity and of mercy, which Judaism never succeeded in propagating to any great extent, either from feebleness of moral purpose, or from defect of sympathy with humanity at large. But without this there is no blessedness for the "families of the earth." Wealth, numbers, military prowess—none of them, nor all of them, can make a nation well and strong, without a moral substratum of character, the feeling of honour, the love of justice, kindness, and truth.

We are disposed to push the question also into the region of the intellect. The Jewish people are endowed with a strong and swift intelligence, and have had a religion which exercised thought, and encouraged the pursuit of knowledge. Yet how little have they attempted for the education of mankind! how little have they even cultivated their own minds in times and in countries where they have not received a stimulus from Christianity!

Let us explain what we mean. We do not at all forget the reputation of the Jews for erudition and the pursuit of certain arts and sciences, at a time when intellectual darkness and lethargy brooded over Europe. We recognize a truth in the proud saying, that "there were no dark ages for Israel." Especially under the caliphs in Spain the Jews were men of letters, and their sons thronged the great schools of Cordova, Toledo, Barcelona, and Grenada. They almost monopolized the profession of medicine, and were proficients in the mathematics and in such astronomy as was cultivated at that time. They made known to Europe the Arabian philosophy, of which Averroes was the great master—a mass of speculation and of comment on Aristotle—which has been fairly enough compared with the Christian Scholasticism. The Sephardim, or Spanish Jews, have the most distinguished history; but in Portugal also, and in Italy, this people cultivated letters and sciences; and by the intelligence which their habits of travelling greatly promoted, and the commercial enterprise which marked them off from the rough and reckless population around them, they gained a disastrous prominence throughout most of the countries of Europe. Disastrous! because it exposed them to jealousy and persecution. Now we have not a word to say in palliation of the shameful cruelty with which so-called Christian governments, instigated by ecclesiastics, and supported by popular fanaticism, drove the Jews from their homes, confiscated their property, and by violence robbed them of their children: not a word, unless it be that which applies to all persecution on religious grounds, that man is an animal that learns very slowly. He has taken thousands of years to climb up to moral truths, which when reached are so obvious, that one cannot comprehend how they were not seen from the beginning; and especially the rights of conscience, the simple principles of religious liberty, have only in these late generations got possession of the human mind, and in many quarters, even in England itself, are not completely understood and acted on even at the present hour. But our indignation is livelier even than our pity, when we think of the bloody cruelty of the Crusaders to the Jews in Germany; or of the conduct of the kings of France, who showed some toleration to the Jews when they wanted money from them, then scouted and expelled them, then allowed them to return only to plunder and banish them again. Our kings of England were little if any better in their conduct to the inoffensive Hebrews who settled in such ancient cities as London, Bristol, and York; and in the time of Edward I., at the desire of Parliament, all the Jews were banished from this realm, with pitiless exactions and ruthless severities. Most monstrous of all these acts of unchristian injustice was the expulsion of the Jews from Spain, under Ferdinand and Isabella, in the year 1492, at the instigation of the infamous Inquisitor-General Torquemada. When we read the story, our sympathy is entirely and warmly with the Jews; and our admiration kindles as we mark the steadfastness of a people who, to the number of hundreds of thousands, sacrificed all that they had, bore every hardship and indignity, and risked every danger, fleeing to Barbary, to Italy, and to the Levant, rather than change their faith at the bidding of their persecutors.

Now, it is only reasonable to infer that so many oppressions and transportations seriously interrupted the pursuit of knowledge by the Jews, and tended to narrow the sympathy of the race. And it is quite fair for the Jew to retort upon us, that if his people, after making acknowledged attainments in various branches of·learning and of practical skill, failed to do anything of importance for the intellectual progress of the world, the blame lies not so much on them as on their Christian tyrants.

We are willing to go further still in ascribing a certain intellectual renown to the Jews. It is the sign of a well-endowed race, that even when the level of culture is not high, they produce a certain proportion of lofty and powerful minds. And, to confine our view to the last 1,000 or even 800 years, we have no difficulty in recognizing such minds among the Jews.

Abraham Ben Ezra, of Toledo, in the twelfth century, was for his time eminent as a commentator, grammarian, philosopher, cabalist, physician, mathematician, astronomer, and poet.

He had a contemporary who is even more famous, Moses Maimonides of Cordova, a disciple of Averroes, who was not only a most distinguished physician, but also a voluminous author in theology, logic, and astronomy. He was too much of a philosopher, however, to be a good traditional Jew.

Don Isaac Abarbanel, born at Lisbon in 1437, was a man of much erudition and wonderful versatility, but of a bitter and haughty spirit. Not unlike him was Manasseh Ben Israel, the eminent linguist and theologian, who came over from Amsterdam to confer with Oliver Cromwell regarding the restoration of the Jews to England,—a project which found favour with the Lord Protector.

Benedict Espinoza is a name which becomes more and more illustrious in the history of abstract thought. He was excommunicated from the synagogue for his opinions; but when we are thinking of great intellects of the Jewish race, we cannot omit one who, judge as we may of his pantheism, must be pronounced one of the most blameless men and profound thinkers in all the annals of philosophy.

And, to mention but one more, Moses Mendelssohn, grandfather of the musical genius, Felix Mendelssohn, did in the last century acquire such distinction throughout Germany as a metaphysical writer, without breaking away, as Spinoza did, from the Jewish theology, that he powerfully influenced public opinion in a direction favourable to his brethren, and raised the Jews out of the obloquy under which they had lain. Mendelssohn revived the speculative, some said the rationalizing, tendency of Maimonides.

We say nothing of the eminent Jewish intellects that have been in the service of Christianity, because we are discussing the intellectual influence of anti-Christian Judaism. And we have cited a few illustrious names to show that we are far from taunting that Judaism with mental barrenness. Yet, after all this, we return unshaken to our position, that not Judaism but Christianity has been the intellectual elevator of the modern world. Whenever and wherever the Jews have been scholars and scientists, we shall find that they have been under another and a stronger intellectual stimulus than their own. In Spain they were impelled towards learning by the Arabian scholars, and encouraged by the Saracen princes. In other countries of Europe they have been influenced by the Christian light that shone around them.

To make this more plain, consider the history of the Jews in those regions where they have not had this light round about them,—*e.g.*, in Persia, in Egypt, in Morocco. They have been for generations sunk in superstition and ignorance. They are Pharisaically religious, and scrupulously observant of Rabbinical ceremonies and dietary regulations. But in what condition are their minds? Education is neglected, and the only mental food which their religion supplies consists of mere shells or husks of Rabbinical commentary and tradition. Now this cannot be ascribed to religious persecution. In some of these lands—notably in the Turkish Empire—the Jews have long enjoyed more favour than any Christians. In days when the Greek or the Armenian had to skulk like a criminal through the streets of Stamboul, the Jew could walk erect and without fear. It is not oppression, it is the pernicious influence of the traditional system in which they are bound, which has hindered the mental development of this people under the protection of the Crescent.

We have not been sparing in our admissions that in many parts of Europe the Jews were grievously wronged by Christians who misconstrued the mind of Christ. Yet we maintain that it is Christianity after all that has given culture to modern Jews, and set them on that course of intellectual improvement which, taken with their remarkable commercial capacity and financial position, gives them a new importance in the world. In Western Europe, and in America, they have so far conformed to Christian ideas as to abandon practices which have been detrimental to the family life of their brethren in the East; and even in Russia, the Rabbinic laws of divorce and early marriage, though in force among the Jews, are gradually falling into discredit. Whatever touches family life touches also the education of the young. Now it is notorious that a great thirst for education has sprung up among English, American, and German Jews. And it is the fashion at present to take special notice of the successes of Jewish students, and to anticipate great things from the Jewish mind, pointing to the part it plays already among the statesmen, jurists, financiers, and journalists of Europe. But to what is the intellectual advance of the modern Jews really due? Have the Rabbinical schools brought about this result ? Is it traditional Talmudic Judaism that has educated the Jew into this fitness to cope with, and even to lead, the Christian ? Assuredly not. It is not too much to say that to be educated and influenced by such Judaism alone is to be doomed to grow up a mere pedant, out of harmony with contemporary thought and life, and quite unfit to exert a real influence upon the world.

It was the Prussian Government that first compelled the Jews to give a useful education to their children. The Rabbis were alarmed. And the boon of a thorough education, which has proved of such service in many ways to the whole German nation, had at first to be forced on the Jewish portion of the population. But it soon came to be appreciated ; and there has followed a great improvement in the education of the Hebrew people in Holland, Italy, England, and elsewhere ; so great an improvement, that there has sprung up a generation of Western Jews wider in culture than any generation that ever went before, and not only qualified to act, but unquestionably acting, with no small effect on the public opinion, and therefore on the course and fortunes of the leading nations of the world. How far this new element is perilous to the Church of God, and is practically an ally of Positivism and Infidelity, is a serious question, which we must not at this time pause to examine. What we maintain is, that the intellectual progress of the modern Jews, and the consequent increase of their influence, are due, not to an impulse from within acting through the dreary formalism of the Rabbinical schools, but to an impulse from without, *i.e.*, from the surrounding Christian civilization acting through schools, lyceums, and universities which Christianity has founded and continues to support. If the modern Jew in Berlin, Paris, or London is quite a citizen of the world, able to join without hesitation in the scientific investigations, literary discussions, and political strifes of the day, it is because he is as little as possible of a Rabbinical Jew, has conformed himself to Christian models, and thrown himself out of the narrow limits of Jewish thought into the broad stream of European civilization.

The sum of our lecture is this, that whether we regard theology, morality, or intellectual life, it is Christianity and not Judaism that has blessed our modern world. We return to the thought that when the Church and the synagogue parted company, two rivers went apart, both tracing their origin to the covenant with Abraham. It seems to us that one of them has singularly failed to irrigate the dry plains of the earth, and is losing much of its water among the sands of materialistic unbelief. The other has sent out branches into almost every land, and, even where its waters have been soiled with admixtures of superstition and error, they have never failed to communicate some blessing as they flowed. Aye, and though this river, too, loses much in the sands of unbelief, it has such vital supplies as to grow wider and fuller and more irresistible in its flow. Respect for woman, family purity, public justice, the love of mercy, the spread of knowledge, the progress of the arts, the noble passion of liberty, all these grow best on the banks of our Christian stream. Jews have them, but have them when they live among Christians, and cannot help breathing a Christian atmosphere.

It is in our hearts to appeal to the enlightened philanthropic Jew. You think of the Almighty God, not as your national Deity merely, but as the God and Father of all. And you have caught the idea and the feeling of humanity. Though your own nation be most properly the first in your eyes, you wish to see all nations blessed in virtue, in peace, in the knowledge of God. Now what religion is in fullest harmony with this aspiration? Is it Judaism, self-contained and non-missionary, laying stress on rites and restrictions which are obviously adapted to an oriental race only, and can never become universal? Or is it Christianity, which contains all the ancient Scriptural revelation that you have in Judaism, and adds a luminous declaration and heart-thrilling proof of God's love to all, binds as many as receive it into one brotherhood, requires no rites that may not with equal facility be adopted and practised by all families of the earth, and has shown an inherent power to root itself in every clime, to elevate the life of every people, to twine with itself the mental and moral progress of the race, to penetrate all social conditions, surmount every barrier, survive and correct the errors of its own administrators, face without fear every new school of human speculation, and steadily move on to conquer and to mould the world?

VI.

The True Prerogative and Glory of the Jews.

BY

THE REV. PROFESSOR BIRKS, M.A.

VI.

THE TRUE PREROGATIVE AND GLORY OF THE JEWS.

THE title of this Lecture implies the previous admission of one or two fundamental truths, apart from which its terms could have no consistent and intelligible meaning.

First, it is assumed that our world is no piece of mere mechanism, but the theatre of a great scheme of moral government and human probation. It is not the slave of physical laws, acting mechanically with irresistible force, beginning we know not how, and tending we know not whither. Men are not machines of a very complex and peculiar kind, condensations of solar force, wrapped up mysteriously, one knows not how, in the convolutions of the brain. They are not automata, in that unnatural sense of the word, which makes it denote the absence of all self-moving power, things pushed and pulled to and fro by environing conditions of existence, without choice or volition of their own. They are beings endued with reason and the power of choice, and responsible to the Supreme Governor of the universe for all their actions. Life is no series of illusions, in which men and nations rise, like bubbles, to the surface of a vast ocean of ceaseless fatal changes, and then burst and disappear. In such a world of slaves or shadows, it would be senseless to claim for any man, or race of men, dignity, prerogative, or glory of any kind. Each of them must bear about with them the brand of a slave, and the clank of their fetters must be heard in every step of their movements. We must assume that all physical laws are only the basement of a lofty edifice, surmounted by laws of a higher kind; moral and spiritual truths, which appeal to the hearts and consciences of men, as made at first in the image of God; and that the architect of the material and outward world is also the Supreme Lord and Governor of the moral universe.

Man is a responsible being. He has a power of choice, which may be, and often is, abused. He has duties which he is bound to fulfil, a law which he ought to obey. Traces of that Divine image, in which he was created at first, still remain, however obscured, and constitute a common prerogative and glory of all mankind. They may debase themselves by brutish lusts and sensual appetites, but still they are not brute beasts, with no understanding for higher things. They are rational and accountable creatures, over whom we may read that Divine message, as a title of honour and a voice of warning—" Every one of us shall give account of himself unto God."

But a second truth is also implied, which does not command universal assent, even among Theists and Christians themselves. Moral duties, and their correlates, moral distinctions, prerogatives, and honours, belong not only to individuals, but to communities, societies, nations, and races of men. Their union with each other, by common descent, and in smaller or larger families, gives rise to a large variety of special duties one towards another, and of all in common towards other families, and the rest of mankind. Union is strength, and with moral agents, added strength is added responsibility. A race or nation have power to do many things, by their combined action, which the separate units could not do. And hence there is a wide range of obligations, which depend on the capacities of men for social and combined action, and apply to all nations, races, or voluntary associations of men. These obligations, when fulfilled, must have their counterpart in common privileges, honours, or tokens of Divine power and blessing. Nor is this the whole truth. He who has made us men, not brutes, by His own good pleasure, has the power and right to vary His own gifts, and to allot variously, to different men or sets of men, special distinctions, gifts and privileges, entrusting more talents to one class, and fewer to another; but all under one common charge, to use them aright for

His glory, and the good of their fellow-creatures, and with the certainty of a later inquiry as to how they have actually been employed.

Here, then, is the starting-point of our inquiry. All men, from our first parents onwards, are actors in a vast scheme of Divine Providence, in which every individual, and every race or nation, has duties to fulfil, a work assigned to them to accomplish, various gifts and talents committed for their use, and privileges and honours of different kinds, which may either be forfeited by abuse, or become fuller, larger, and more complete, when recognised as a sacred trust from the Giver of all good things, and rightly improved. Is there any such privilege which belongs to the Jewish race and people? If they had such a privilege in the times of their national greatness, does it still continue, or has it come utterly to an end? Or is the truth somewhere between these limits? What if the prerogative and honour of the Jewish people is, like the Jewish damsel of old, in a state of suspended animation, but not of utter death, so that it may be said with truth, " The damsel is not dead, but sleepeth," and a voice of power may soon go forth, in which it may revive once more, partake of the food of life, and stand forth before the world in all the beauty of a life from which the shadows of the grave have passed away, and on which there will rest the clear light of the manifest blessing of heaven?

There is a great scheme of Providence, carried on from age to age in our world, of which God is the author, the subjects the whole race of mankind through successive generations, and the aim and purpose, redemption and recovery from the bondage of moral evil of ever-increasing numbers of souls, to heights, ever unfolding more and more, of life, immortality, Holy happiness, communion with God, and everlasting felicity. The true privilege and honour of any child of man is, first, to be the receiver of a share in the benefits of this great redemption ; and next, to be a chosen instrument, in the hand of God, for the larger unfolding and wider spread of these heavenly blessings. Nearness of union with God Himself, first, as the receiver of His gifts, and next, and still more, as a fellow-worker in His great plan of love, is the only true standard of prerogative, dignity, and honour, in the sight of heaven. All honours apart from this are mere shadows, and, in proportion as the Divine plan unfolds itself more fully, will disappear like the dreams of a night vision.

Again, the highest form of privilege and honour cannot belong to any race of men, or corporate body of men, but to individuals alone. For God's highest gifts to men are those which apply to them as personal moral agents, who must bear each his own burden, give account for his own works, and have a direct and immediate relation of union and fellowship with the great Author of his moral being. The personal, individual life is that which is innermost and deepest in man's complex and many-sided existence. Nearness to God, in a community, can only result from the nearness of individual members of that community, through whom, by association, the rest are raised into an intimacy they could not otherwise have attained. To drink in the words and messages of God, to experience their quickening power in the deepest chambers of the heart, to be set free by them from the dominion and curse of sin, to be renewed in the image of the Creator, and then to co-operate, consciously and willingly, in the great work of redemption, for which the whole system of the universe is sustained, is the highest of all privileges. It cannot belong to any one, either by birth, as descended from any special stock or race, nor by the will of men, associating in any voluntary fellowship, but by a direct work of Divine adoption, which is not and cannot be given in a crowd, or to men as parts and fractions of a community; but to such moral agents, one by one, as if standing alone in the presence, and under the gracious eye, of the King of heaven. And thus, to the Jew under the Old Testament, to be a true servant and worshipper of the God of Israel, admitted to nearness of communion with Him, was a higher privilege than simple membership in the family of Israel, however great and manifold the favour shown to God's peculiar people.

What, then, is the standard of these privileges by which one race or people may be honourably distinguished from another? It is the intimacy of their relation to God's great plan of redemption, and the special post or office assigned them in connection with the final aim of universal Providence; in modern phrase, the greatest happiness of the greatest number, but in words more truly appropriate to describe it, the glory of God in the spiritual and eternal salvation of men.

Now the same Scriptures, which reveal to us the unbroken constancy of this great scheme of Divine love and mercy from the days of Paradise until now, reveal it, from first to last, in most intimate connection with the people of Israel. Let us trace briefly the connection, in the times of the Old Testament, from Moses to Malachi, in the days of the Gospels, in the past eighteen centuries of Jewish dispersion and captivity, and in the hopes and promises made to Israel in the days to come.

The Old Testament, the writings of Moses and the Prophets, entrusted to the Jewish people as the oracles of the living God, contain a long series of promises of good things to come, all connected with a Person, dimly announced at first, and more clearly when the ages moved on, as the future Deliverer of mankind from the bitter consequences of their own wilful departure from the law and command of God. He is the Seed of the woman who is promised to bruise the head of the serpent, receiving himself a bruise in the great moral conflict; the Seed of Abraham, in whom all nations are to be blest; the Shiloh, the Prince of Peace, to whom all nations are to be gathered; the Lamb whom God would provide for a burnt offering; the Prophet like unto Moses, to whom his people should give ear; the Son of David, the Son of the Virgin, the Anointed Servant of the Lord, the Man whose name is the Branch, the Shepherd of Israel, the Lord, pierced by his own people, the Man who is Jehovah's fellow, the Angel of the Covenant, the Sun of Righteousness, to rise upon his people with healing in his wings. All the various rays of promise, and voices of prophetic hope, converge in this one great object from first to last. Whether Jesus of Nazareth is the person in which these promises all meet, or, in the words of the Baptist, we need still to look for another, is the great question at issue between Judaism and Christianity. But that the writings of Moses and the Prophets, the sacred Scriptures of the Jews, do contain such a series of statements, connected most intimately with the hopes they reveal of future times of restitution, deliverance, and blessing, is a patent fact to all who read them with an intelligent mind and unbiassed heart. Testimony to the reality, person, and work of a coming Messiah, through whom God's purposes of grace towards our world are to be at length fulfilled, is the burden and sum of their message through four thousand years. It runs onward from the voice to the serpent, " It shall bruise thy head, and thou shalt bruise his heel," to the parting promise, veiled under the noblest symbol the physical world can supply,—" Unto you that fear my name shall the Sun of Righteousness arise, with healing in his wings."

Now every step in this long chain of promised mercies, and each new development of the hope of the Messiah, is linked closely and inseparably with the history of the Jewish people. Their very birth, as a nation, was inwrought with one leading promise of the coming Redeemer of the world. When it was said to Abraham, " In thy seed shall all the families of the earth be blessed," the promise might seem to apply, either to Messiah in person, or to the family amongst whom he was to appear, as descended from Abraham. They are set apart, by a solemn consecration at Sinai, to receive a series of messages, which contain the unfolding of the great purpose of Divine wisdom and love. In the midst of a world fast sinking into gross idolatry they are made the depositaries of a pure and lofty Theism. The code of laws provided for them bears the impress of this great truth, that there is one God, and none other but He; that to forsake and deny Him is the foremost of all evils, and that to worship and serve Him with the whole heart and mind and strength, is more than all burnt offering and sacrifice, the first and great commandment, the chief duty and highest privilege of man.

All the gifts bestowed on the Jewish people, and recorded in the sacred history for a thousand years, are summed up in the fact that they were stewards, trustees, and depositaries of the great hope of a coming redemption for all the rest of mankind. The promised Saviour of the world, the Beginner of the new creation, the Author of the good things to come, was to be specially the hope and the glory of Israel. From their race he was to spring. In Bethlehem, the city of David, he was to be born. The law which the Jews had received through Moses, their great prophet and the founder of their nation, was the discipline under which he was to be trained. He was to magnify it, and make it honourable, by his own obedience. All the rays of light in the Old Testament, which meet on the head of the promised Messiah, pass through an atmosphere of history, prophecy, type and figure, commands and promises, all steeped in Jewish associations, and connected with the sacred records of the history of Israel. The morning beams of the Sun of Righteousness are all coloured with Jewish colouring, when he is set before us in the last of the Jewish prophets, as about to rise upon our dark and benighted world with healing in his wings.

Such was the great privilege and chief glory of the Jewish people, all through the fourteen or fifteen centuries of the Old Testament, from the time of the first passover to the Christian era and the last of the Asmonæan kings. What light is thrown on this subject by the momentous changes of those seventy years, which include the rise of Christianity, the downfall of the Temple, and the dispersion of the Jewish people?

In the view of Christians, the privilege and glory of the Jews did not then cease, but rather attained its more complete development. The hope and expectation became an accomplished reality. What Jewish prophets and kings had long desired and wished for was at last fulfilled. And this fulfilment, while it realized their best hopes, went beyond them, and revealed a mystery of Divine love and wisdom, so grand and glorious, that it could only be dimly guessed at before it was actually realized. The Word, the Maker of all things, was made flesh, and tabernacled among us. He whose goings forth were from of old, even from everlasting, was born at Bethlehem. The long series of prophetic hopes and promises, of which the Jewish people had been made the chosen trustees for all mankind, were fulfilled in a way which crowned and completed the honourable pre-eminence given to them among all people and nations on the face of the earth. The truth finds its condensed expression in the words of the great

Apostle himself—a Hebrew of Hebrews, and brought up after the strictest severity of the Jewish faith. He thus describes the privileges divinely bestowed on his own people, " Who are Israelites, to whom pertaineth the adoption, and the glory, and the covenants, and the giving of the law, and the promises ; whose are the fathers, and of whom as concerning the flesh Christ hath come, who is over all, God blessed for ever, Amen."

Here, then, as taught by the lips of the Apostle, and re-echoed by the deep instincts of every Christian heart, is the crowning privilege of the Jews as a people, and the special honour assured to them by the sovereign will and firm decree of the God of heaven, who is also, by a special title, the God of Israel.

Let us consider the great facts of the New Testament in their bearing on the privilege or dishonour, the glory or the shame, of the Jewish people, under four different views which have been and are still held as to their real character.

First, let us examine the view of the main body of the Jewish people for many ages, and of some eminent unbelievers of our own times, that Jesus of Nazareth was an impostor and a blasphemer, who deceived the people, either by false pretences to miraculous powers, or else by miracles wrought by magic, and compact with the powers of darkness. Such, in substance is the view upheld by one celebrated modern poet, in the "Revolt of Islam," that Christianity is one more instance of new weapons supplied by darkness, in the cycles of revolving years, to the powers of evil. In this case the appearance of Jesus of Nazareth, and the later success of His religion, would be a deep and indelible disgrace to the whole people amidst whom the delusion arose. A Jewish deceiver, sustaining his pretensions by the ambiguous words of Jewish prophets, propagating falsehood by Jewish disciples, would have effected a reign of falsehood and delusion on the largest scale, and thereby impressed a strange and mournful character on the whole history of the world, for near two thousand years. The rich melodies of the songs of Zion will find their only issue in a terrible and hateful discord. A long series of Divine messages, rich in noblest thoughts and varied utterances of sublime and lofty hope, will have issued in something worse than mere disappointment and vexation of spirit. They will have their final result, on the one hand, in the scattering, distress, and desolation of the chosen people, lasting through long ages; and on the other, in the birth and growth of the most gigantic and astonishing fraud, which has ever interfered with the growth and progress of genuine science, or distorted, hindered, and disturbed the progress of the human race to its destined goal of truth, wisdom, and love. Once accept this dark view of Christianity and its Founder, and men of every tribe may point at the Jew the finger of scorn, and say, "You are the one race and people who have brought upon our race the greatest of calamities. We asked for bread, and you have given us a stone; we asked for a fish, and you have given us a serpent. You led us by the books you revere, and the writers whom you uphold to have been true messengers from the God of heaven, to look for some great Deliverer to spring from your race, in whom all families of the earth should receive a large and full blessing. Instead of this, what have you given us? A false creed, a subtle deceiver, a gigantic birth of fraud and delusion, growing more colossal in stature, and wider in range, year by year, the fruits of which have been, to yourselves, countless persecutions, to the world, an immense increase of superstition, idolatry, and spiritual delusions; and the delay, for long ages, of the hoped-for regeneration of our race, and the triumph of liberty, wisdom, peace, and love."

But the same view of the facts of the Gospel, which turns them from the chief honour and glory of the Jewish people, unto their greatest reproach and shame, involves also a moral problem impossible to solve without a denial of the moral government of the world, or else making God himself an accomplice in the work of fraud and delusion. For the history parts the Jewish people into two classes,—those who received and accepted the claim of Jesus of Nazareth to be the true Messiah, and those by whom it was rejected and disowned. And that is the double fact, in the later history, which has to be explained. On this view, the class and party among the Jews who were faithful to the trust they had received from the God of Israel, refused the claims of an impostor to be the Messiah of God, who punished him for blasphemies which the law of God condemned, · and clung to the genuine hope of their own prophets, though long delayed ; have ever since been outcasts, fugitives, persecuted, wandering to and fro through the earth, the crown fallen from their head, combining strangely the righteousness of Abel with the curse of Cain, a proverb of reproach and a byeword through long ages of dispersion and shame. On the other hand, those who adopted the delusion, who countenanced and even worshipped the Deceiver who had risen within the sacred bounds of Israel, have thriven and prospered, both in numbers, intellectual gifts, and worldly prosperity. The mightiest nations of the earth, through long ages, have accepted their teaching, and ranged themselves on their side. They have wrought a complete revolution in the institutions, morals, and habits of one-fourth of the whole human race, and of that fourth which has power and influence beyond all the rest. Is not this, indeed, a marvellous paradox, an enigma most strange and unaccountable and incredible, that the God of heaven should single out one nation, for a thousand years, to be special depositaries and stewards of Divine messages, and then at last, out of the bosom of this very people, there should arise, not the fulfilment of the glorious hopes He had kindled in the hearts of men, but a gigantic counterfeit and delusion, receiving through long ages all the outward signs of blessing from above; while those who have faithfully withstood the progress of error, and kept the old landmarks of Moses and the prophets, have suffered exile, dispersion, imprisonment, and troubles almost unexampled in the history of mankind. On this view of the true character of the history of Jesus of Nazareth, not only a deep reproach, instead of honour, rests on the Jewish people as a whole, but the opposite issues, in the case of the believers in the crucified Nazarene, and the rejectors of his claims, imperil our faith in the moral government of the world, and would almost imply that an evil power, friendly to imposture, and the enemy of righteousness, has determined the outlines of the world's history for the last two thousand years.

Let us now consider an hypothesis less extreme, though far unlike the faith of Christians, which many Jews less rigid than their fathers, and some philosophers, have espoused within the last fifty years. The Reformer of Galilee is not to be defamed as a mere impostor, nor yet to be honoured as a Prophet, but regarded as a sincere enthusiast, bent on the liberation of the poor from the oppression of the rich and mighty, and full of a generous sympathy for the sorrows and distresses of mankind. He was not a deceiver, but honestly self-deceived. He persuaded himself, and strove to persuade others, that he was the Messiah whom his people expected, and of whom the prophets wrote. And when the opposition of the rulers made him despair of immediate success, he laid down his life by a kind of voluntary suicide, rather than confess his error, or abandon his purpose, and confess that events had disproved his claims. Thus at the last, the noble enthusiast in the cause of humanity passed from self-deception into the unworthy task of deceiving others, but his faults are to be condoned from the loftiness of his aim.

On this view of the character of Jesus, the dishonour his course, and the success of his creed, reflects on the Jewish people, is less aggravated, but not less real, than before. The history of the nation from Abraham onward, through near two thousand years, the long series of Divine messages given to Jewish prophets, so grand in conception, so rich and various in the elements of lofty hope, spiritual aspiration, and promises of heavenly blessing, reduce themselves to a melancholy illustration of the proverb, " Whoso boasteth himself of a false gift is like clouds and wind without rain." The issue of what assumes to be a vast continuous scheme of Divine revelation, carried on for fifteen hundred years, would be to have promised much and performed nothing, and to have wakened high hopes in the minds of men only to dash them to the earth when the time of their fulfilment seemed to have come, and thus to have trifled with and disappointed the deepest instincts of the heart and the noblest aspirations of mankind. The children ask for bread, and their heavenly Father gives them a stone, the mere dreams of a mistaken enthusiast, and not the living bread that cometh down from heaven. On the other view, examined before, the case is still worse, and they receive a serpent. On either view the Jewish people must share largely in the reproach which is cast upon God himself, by the frustration of His own messages of hope and comfort to mankind. He has said, and has not done it. He has spoken, and will not make it good. The eyes of His people have failed with longing for a promised Messiah, who never appears, and a dreaming enthusiast comes in His stead, who deludes millions on millions of mankind with visionary hopes and promises, which have no real warrant from the God of heaven.

A third view of the facts of the gospel may be taken, and is not quite so wide of the truth as the two others. Jesus was not indeed the Son of God, come down from heaven. But he was a prophet sent with a message from God, and greater than all who had gone before. This is the view held by all the followers of Islam, with the further addition, that one prophet, still greater, has since appeared, and now claims the allegiance and submission, to his later message, of all mankind. Such a view, it is true, cannot be reconciled with the historical truth of the narratives in the four Gospels. If Jesus were a mere man, and said what he is reported to have said, and did what he is reported to have done, the charge of a blasphemous claim to Divine honour, on which he is said to have been condemned by the Jewish rulers, would have been clearly proved. The sentence pronounced against him would have been just, however severe. But, setting aside this great difficulty, and moulding the facts to suit this mitigated Christianity of Mahometans and Unitarians, the appearance of Christ and the success of his religion would be an honour to the Jewish people, and not a disgrace. It would add one more to the long list of spiritual benefits which they have been entrusted with—the high privilege of receiving in trust themselves, and then of transmitting, as honoured stewards, to the other nations of the earth.

But while this view of the Christian message does not deprive the Jew of all honour, and turn his glory into shame, one result at least is clear. It abolishes his primacy, and deposes him from the first to only a secondary place in the scale of national privilege. If the Son of Mary were a great prophet, succeeded by one still greater, the son of Abdallah, and the New

Testament, after supplementing Moses and the Prophets, has in turn been supplemented by the Koran, the children of Ishmael must replace the sons of Israel in the station of highest honour in the spiritual history of the world. The prerogative may still remain with the seed of Abraham, the common forefather of the Jews and the tribes of the Arabian desert. But the relative order in Genesis is reversed. The son of the bondwoman takes precedence of the son of the free woman, and the child who was born after the flesh outstrips in spiritual dignity him who was born in spirit, and by promise. The honour of the Jewish people may still be great, from the long series of Divine messengers who have appeared among them. But the latest will have cast all the others into the shade, and transferred the pre-eminence to another tribe and race, the Hashemites of Arabia, to whom, if this doctrine were true, the place of highest honour will have been allotted among the various tribes of mankind by the sovereign will of heaven.

But let us now turn to the fourth and last view of the New Testament history, which has been embodied in the faith of Christians in every age. Jesus of Nazareth is no impostor, deceiving others, or enthusiast self-deceived, but the great Prophet who was to come into the world—the Messiah of God. And this is not the whole truth. This Prophet, who sums up and completes the message of a long series who have gone before, is no mere man invested with special gifts and miraculous powers : He is the Son of God, come down from heaven. He is the Word of God, by whom all things were created, and without whom was not made one single thing that has been made. He is Emmanuel, which means, being interpreted, God with us. He is the Lord, the messenger or angel of the covenant, who bears the name Jehovah, and before whom, as the Lord God, a messenger was sent to prepare the way. His coming was the crown of a long series of Divine privileges and honours which the people of Israel had received through long ages, summed up in those impressive and solemn words, " Whose are the fathers, and of whom as concerning the flesh Christ came, who is over all, God blessed for ever."

The incarnation, as it is the foundation-stone of the Christian faith, is also the crown and top-stone of the privileges and honours of the people of Israel. For what does this doctrine imply ? All the laws of nature, and all physical changes, are only the basement and pedestal of a vast scheme of Divine Providence, which includes in its structure all moral and spiritual truths, and a full unfolding of the glorious attributes of the Creator, and of which the scope and aim is the redemption of innumerable souls, to be renewed in God's image, and made supremely blessed in His love for evermore. All the earlier steps of this great scheme are set before us in the Scriptures of the Old Testament, Moses and the Prophets, and centre in the hope of a coming Redeemer of the world. These hopes were conveyed to the rest of mankind through messages given first to Israel, and the voices of Jewish prophets from age to age. A hundred various types, in ordinances of the Jewish law, and the persons of Jewish lawgivers, priests, judges, prophets, and kings, centre in the person of the promised Messiah, who was to be the seed of Abraham, and the Son of David, and through whom a large blessing was assured to all the nations of the earth. But the Old Testament, amidst the rich and varied harmonies of the songs of Zion, has throughout its whole course one great unresolved discord. It denounces from first to last the sin of idolatry, as most abominable in the sight of God, and lays down his solemn decision, " I am the Lord, that is my name, and my glory I will not give to another." Yet, side by side with these statements and warnings, it contains a series of messages, which teach the people of God to look forward with eager desire to the coming of the promised Messiah, as one born of woman, who was to be the object of their deepest affection and most intense longing, and in whose name they were to trust. This discord, so strange at first sight, finds its solution in the great mystery of the Christian faith. Messiah, the Son of man, is also the Son of the living God: his name is Emmanuel, God with us. God has been manifested in the flesh. In the words of Micah, One would be born at Bethlehem, "whose goings forth have been from of old, even from everlasting."

Man's true place in creation is not to be a little higher than the ape, but a little lower than the angels. But the highest glory of our human nature is one which even the angels do not share. It is the mysterious truth that the Son of God, the world's Redeemer, took not on him the nature of angels, but our own. And this marvel of Divine love is linked inseparably with the special honour and prerogative of the Jewish people. He took on him "the seed of Abraham." The Word was made flesh, and made flesh in the royal line of the house of David. The Son of the Most High God became the son of a Jewish mother. His birthplace was a village of Judea. His childhood and youth were one long training in obedience to the Jewish law. The notes which resound at every step of his history are such as these: "Where is he that is born King of the Jews?" "He shall reign over the house of Jacob for ever." "Glad tidings of great joy, which shall be to all the people." "I am not sent save to the lost sheep of the house of Israel." "Hosanna to the Son of David." "Blessed be the King of Israel which cometh in the name of the Lord." "This is Jesus, the King of the Jews." "Neither shalt thou swear by Jerusalem, for it is the city of the great King." From the cradle to the grave, every title of mystery and ascription of reverence to the world's Redeemer overflows also with undertones of privilege, honour, and blessing for his brethren after the flesh, the chosen race and line amongst whom he was to be born, beloved for the sake of the fathers.

Through long ages the sons of Israel have failed to see, or refused to own, the greatest of all the many gifts of honour and national distinction which they have received from the sovereign bounty of God. The most precious jewel in their diadem, the choicest and most unfading flower in the chaplet which the supreme King of nations has prepared for their brows, has been ignominiously cast away. In cleaving to the traditions of the Talmud, many of them very childish, and refusing to own the Messiahship of Jesus of Nazareth, and the further and deeper truth, that the long-promised Saviour was no mere man, however good or wise, but the Son of God come down from heaven, they have sorrowfully fulfilled the saying of their own prophet, uttered when he was rehearsing in his own history a great type of the coming redemption, "They that choose lying vanities forsake their own mercies." How we should long for the time when the veil which has rested on their eyes so long shall be taken away, and all of them shall adopt the confession of the true Israelite, when a word of Divine insight revealed to him the secrets of his life and hidden experience: "Rabbi, thou art the Son of God, thou art the King of Israel!"

But scarcely less strange and wonderful than this refusal of the Jewish people to recognize the most astonishing of the many honours God has bestowed upon them, is the treatment they have received, for long ages, from the professed followers of Christ, of which many sad traces continue even to the present day. All Christians profess to believe that salvation is of the Jew, and that it is from Jewish prophets and apostles they have received the word of eternal life; nay, that He whom they adore as the Saviour of the world, the everlasting Son of the Father, is a Jew by descent, and has sprung from the race of Israel. They believe and profess that it is a Jew, to whom, by Divine decree, all power is given in heaven and earth, and who receives a full tribute of praise and worship from ten thousand times ten thousand angels around the throne of heaven. Yet, how have the Jews been maltreated and despised by these Christians! What reproaches and contumely they have endured! what sufferings of every kind, from those who have claimed to be disciples of the Lord Jesus! Their faith in Him, degenerating into utter superstition, has led them to make his virgin mother, a Jewess of the line of David, a modern Ashtaroth, a new Queen of heaven, the object of a heathenish and idolatrous worship. Surely there is no stranger or sadder spectacle in the whole history of the world, than these two facts, standing side by side for many generations, Divine honour heaped by Christians upon a Jewish maid, under the unscriptural, man-invented title of the Mother of God, and cruel, bitter persecution, by the same Christians, of the whole people to whom this maiden belonged, and amidst whom she was born.

During all those ages, the honour which God had given to the Jewish people, when his own Son, the brightness of his glory, took human flesh of a Jewish mother, was made subject to the Jewish law, and grew up as a root out of dry ground, in the midst of the Jewish people, and in despised Galilee, did not cease and could not pass away. The gifts and calling of God are without repentance. But the highest and choicest benefits and bounties of God depend, to be completely realized, on the co-operation of the human will. In Messiah's works of temporal mercy, the method of their performance, sometimes expressed, always implied, was this, "Believe ye that I am able to do this? According to your faith be it unto you." The Jews have complained, loudly and justly, of the reproach, contempt, and persecution they have endured for ages from those who have called themselves disciples of Christ. And still they have continued to inflict on themselves a deeper wrong than all they have endured from others. If this strange and unnatural blindness is some day to cease, prayer for spiritual light, like that of Bartimeus, must first be offered up to the Lord whom they have rejected, and receive a gracious answer, and the Spirit of grace and supplication be poured out on all the remaining families of Israel. They must fulfil the description of the prophet, and mourn in secret places for their own pride and the pride of their fathers, "all the families that remain, every family apart, and their wives apart."

This great and glorious privilege of the Jewish people, however hidden from their own eyes by unbelief, or forgotten and denied by nominal Christians in years of gross idolatry and hateful persecution, cannot be set aside or made void by the neglect, ignorance, or perverseness of men. It is inwoven into the whole texture of the great scheme of redemption from first to last. When we compare the prophecies both of the Old Testament and the New with the past history and present state of the Jews, we see, on the largest scale, solemn warnings of judgment signally and exactly fulfilled. And this fulfilment of many threatenings is a sure pledge of the fulfilment, in their own time, with equal exactness, of the rich and various promises which accompany these threatenings, blessings assured to the whole house of Israel and Judah, in their day of national repentance and of godly sorrow. Their special relationship to the promised Messiah has not ceased, and can never cease. He announces his own thoughts of deep love towards them, even when exalted at the right hand of the Father in heaven. "For Zion's sake I will not hold my peace, and for Jerusalem's sake I will not rest, until the righteousness thereof go forth as brightness, and the salvation thereof as a lamp that burneth." Their own fervent prayers to the God of grace are the needed signal that the long arrest on the outflow of Divine power towards them may cease, and the mercies of God, in full tide of blessing, visit them once more. They are still "beloved for the fathers' sake." When their self-righteousness shall cease, and the ornament of a broken heart, a meek and quiet spirit, shall be seen in them, they will then be beloved, not only for the fathers' sake, but for their own, and most of all for His sake, who is the true King of Israel. They are the chosen seed, singled out from the rest of mankind, from whom the world's great Redeemer was to be born. And that Redeemer is no other than the Eternal Word, by whom all things were created, the brightness of the Father's glory, in whose Divine person there are unsearchable riches of goodness, wisdom, and love. The curse on those who have rejected or denied this great truth, and the sin which suspends or reverses the blessings that should naturally flow from it, is to the third and fourth generation. But the blessing of their father's covenant is to a thousand generations, and has never yet been exhausted or fulfilled. When in the words of Moses they confess their iniquity, and the iniquity of their fathers, and the trespass by which they have grievously sinned against their God, and mourn for their own and their fathers' sins with deep and genuine repentance, then at last the mercies of God will return to them, and His covenant be fulfilled, when He shall take 'away their sins.

The repentance of a whole nation for national sins is always a hard and difficult thing. Even now we have before our eyes the spectacle of nations, nominally Christian, and even claiming to be patterns of Christian orthodoxy, on whom a sore judgment of God for their idolatry has lighted for four hundred years, and who seem, at the close, as mad upon their idols, as corrupt in their worship, as when the woe first lighted upon them. We see fierce wrath against the instruments of their punishment, and utter unconsciousness of the sin for which it was sent, and not only unchanged idolatry in their own worship, but the same readiness as before to persecute the brethren of that Lord whom they profess to adore. We are told by Ezekiel that wild beasts are one of God's four sore judgments. How much easier do men find it to rail against these wild beasts, or the God of holy judgment who looses them to destroy, than to discover and renounce the sins which bring down the terrible judgment!

Now this, which is true, and seen before our eyes

in the case of Christian nations, not wholly excluding our own, is true also of the people of Israel. But the blindness will not last for ever. Amidst all the dark clouds of oppression, discontent, and degrading superstition, there are already streaks of light in the eastern skies, which shew that a new era of the world's history is close at hand, and will soon begin. In times like these a few years may effect great and surprising changes. The outer court of God's Providence has to do with all the revolutions of earthly kingdoms, by which they minister to God's wonderful counsel of redeeming love. And in this outer court of Providence, soon or late, Israel must hold the foremost place, because their relation is more close and intimate than that of any other race or people to the person of the world's Redeemer. Jesus Christ, our Lord, is also the son of David, and the son of Abraham. This truth, in the opening sentence of the New Testament, is like a keynote to the whole message which follows. It links the gospel with all the earlier histories of the Old Testament, with the sad mystery of the broken covenant, the house overthrown and ruined, the people outcast, the land left waste and desolate, and with the blessings still to come, when God shall visit His people in mercy once more, and largest blessings shall be given to them, and through them to the whole world. Then the words of the Apostle shall crown and complete the message of the earlier prophets,—"And so all Israel shall be saved, as it is written, there shall come out of Zion the Deliverer, and shall turn away ungodliness from Jacob: for this is my covenant with them, when I shall take away their sins." The true Joseph will reveal to his brethren after the flesh the depths of his Divine compassion, and they will then understand, as they have never understood till now, and the world will understand also, what is the chief prerogative and highest honour of the Jewish people. It is their nearness by descent, to Him, who is the great centre of universal Providence, and the Sun of righteousness to the whole of the moral and spiritual universe, Jesus Christ our Lord. "He that scattereth Israel will gather them and keep them as a shepherd doth his flock." Their land will be once more, as of old, "the glory of all lands," and in their restored honour and blessing will be seen the most conspicuous sign of the unchanging truth and goodness of the Lord. When once the people of the Jews, from the proudest become the humblest of all nations, their privileges will return to them in amplest measure, and chief among them will be their manifested nearness to the Saviour, who is the meek and lowly Son of God. "For whosoever exalteth himself shall be abased, but he that humbleth himself shall be exalted."

This is the universal law and method of God's moral government, and must be fulfilled, as in all beside, so pre-eminently in His dealings with Israel, the beloved and chosen people. For "before honour is humility." Their deep humiliation and godly sorrow will be the sure signal for their recovered honour and abiding fulness of blessing.

Printed by Hazell, Watson, and Viney, London and Aylesbury.

The Christian Evidence Society's Lectures.

I.

Ninth Edition. Crown 8vo, cloth. Price 7s. 6d.

MODERN SCEPTICISM.

With an Explanatory Paper by the Right Rev. C. J. ELLICOTT, D.D., Lord Bishop of Gloucester and Bristol.

Contributors — The Lord Archbishop of York, the Lord Bishop of Carlisle, the Lord Bishop of Ely, the Dean of Canterbury, Rev. Canon Cook, Professor Stanley Leathes, M.A., Professor George Rawlinson, M.A., Rev. Prebendary C. A. Row, M.A., Rev. W. Jackson, M.A., F.S.A., Rev. H. Rigg, D.D., Rev. John Stoughton, D.D.

II.

Fourth Edition. Crown 8vo, cloth. Price 7s. 6d.

FAITH AND FREE THOUGHT.

With a Preface by the late Right Rev. SAMUEL WILBERFORCE, D.D., Lord Bishop of Winchester.

Contributors—Sir Bartle Frere, G.C.S.I., K.C.B., D.C.L., the Very Rev. the Dean of Ely, Rev. Canon Mozley, D.D., Rev. Professor Birks, M.A., Charles Brooks, Esq., M.A., Professor J. H. Gladstone, F.R.S., Rev. T. P. Boultbee, LL.D., W. R. Cooper, Esq., Rev. Henry Allon, D.D., Benjamin Shaw, Esq., M.A., and the Rev. Joseph Angus, D.D.

III.

Second Edition. Cloth. Price 2s. 6d.

STRIVINGS FOR THE FAITH.

Lectures Delivered in the Hall of Science, City Road.

Contributors — Rev. Professor Birks, M.A., Rev. Prebendary Row, M.A., Rev. G. F. Maclear, D.D., Rev. J. H. Titcomb, M.A., Rev. Professor Lorimer, D.D., W. R. Browne, M.A., Rev. John Gritton, and B. Harris Cowper, Esq.

THE BAMPTON LECTURES FOR 1875.

Second Edition. Demy 8vo. Price 10s. 6d.

THE DOCTRINE OF RETRIBUTION.
PHILOSOPHICALLY CONSIDERED.

By the REV. W. JACKSON, M.A., F.S.A.,
Formerly Fellow of Worcester College.

"The lectures show an enormous amount of philosophical reading and study, and might almost be described as an eloquent and able series of deductions from the main position of Kant's Philosophy. They abound in acute remarks and striking passages, and will richly repay careful and repeated study."—*Literary Churchman.*

LONDON: HODDER & STOUGHTON, 27, PATERNOSTER ROW.

A POPULAR EXPOSITION of the EPISTLES TO THE SEVEN CHURCHES IN ASIA.

By the Rev. E. H. PLUMTRE, D.D.,

Professor of Theology, King's College, London, and Prebendary of St. Paul's; Author of "Biblical Studies," and Editor of "Cassell's Bible Educator," etc.

In Crown 8vo.   Price 5s.

THE CHRISTIAN CREED.

By the Rev. STANLEY LEATHES, M.A.,

Prebendary of St. Paul's, and Professor of Hebrew, King's College, London; Author of "The Gospel its own Witness," etc.

A Series of Discourses on the Articles of THE APOSTLES' CREED, designed with special reference to the difficulties of modern thought, but popular and practical in treatment.

In Crown 8vo.   Price 7s. 6d.

THE CROSS OF CHRIST.

Studies in the History of Religion and the Inner Life of the Church.

By the Rev. OTTO ZOECKLER, D.D.

Prof. of Theology in Griefswald.   Translated with the co-operation of the Author,

By Rev. MAURICE J. EVANS, B.A.

CONTENTS :—The Cross in the Heathen World, and under the Old Covenant: (1) as a Symbol of Blessing, (2) a Symbol of the Curse.—The Cross of Cavalry according to the Gospels and the Teaching of the Apostles.—The Cross in the pre-Constantine Age.—Constantine's Vision of the Cross, and the Influence thereof upon Mediæval Christianity.—The Cross in the Church of the Middle Ages.—The Spiritual Idea of the Cross as afresh apprehended in the Reformation.—The place of the Cross in the present and future of the Church.

APPENDICES :—The merely ornamental use of the Symbol of the Cross upon pre-Christian monuments.—The symbolical meaning of the Egyptian Ansate Cross.—The site of the Lost Paradise.—The single external circumstances and actions in the work of Crucifixion.—Etc., etc.

In 8vo.   Cloth, 12s.

LONDON : HODDER & STOUGHTON, 27, PATERNOSTER ROW.

EXPOSITORY ESSAYS AND DISCOURSES.

By the Rev. SAMUEL COX,

Editor of "The Expositor," etc., etc.

"This volume is the third of a series of which the 'The Expositor's Note-book' is the first, and 'Biblical Expositions' the second. Like the earlier volumes, which have met with such a cordial reception, it deals, for the most part, with obscure or difficult scriptures, and seeks to explain and vindicate them."

In crown 8vo.   Price 8s. 6d.

SACRED STREAMS.

THE ANCIENT AND MODERN HISTORY OF THE RIVERS OF THE BIBLE.

By PHILIP HENRY GOSSE, F.R.S.

With Forty-four Illustrations and a Map. A New Edition, Revised by the Author.

The rivers and streams of Palestine and the neighbouring lands, hallowed by their being mentioned in the Holy Scriptures, are the subjects of this volume. The author takes each of these in geographical order; describes its topography, botany, and zoology, from the best authorities; recounts the incidents and the scenes of its ancient history, especially such as are recorded in the sacred Word; and pursues its associations, wherever this is instructive, down to modern ages.

In Crown 8vo.   7s. 6d.; gilt edges, 8s.

CHRISTIAN LIFE AND PRACTICE IN THE EARLY CHURCH.

By E. DE PRESSENSÉ, D.D.

Translated by ANNIE HARWOOD-HOLMDEN.

This is the fourth and last volume of a series in which, under the general title of "Early Years of Christianity," M. de Pressensé has given a history of the growth and development of thought, faith, and practice during the first three centuries of the Christian era. The earlier volumes have been some time before the public both in England and France; the closing volume has been delayed owing to the numerous public engagements of the author, and now appears almost simultaneously in both countries. Its general purport is to show how the faith sealed with the blood of martyrs and apologists became, in spite of opposition without, and heresy within, a mighty transforming power in the ancient world; how it quietly undermined slavery, elevated and purified family life, modified legislation, and vindicated true spiritual worship. The book abounds in graphic descriptions of the public and private life of the early Christians, all the details being verified by quotations from contemporary writers, from the "apostolical constitution," or from the latest discoveries in the catacombs.

In Demy 8vo.   Price 12s.

LONDON: HODDER & STOUGHTON, 27, PATERNOSTER ROW.

LETTERS TO A YOUNG CLERGYMAN.

By JOHN C. MILLER, D.D.,
Canon-residentiary of Rochester, Rural Dean and Vicar of Greenwich, Examining Chaplain to the Lord Bishop of Rochester.

In Crown 8vo.   Price 5s.   [Preparing.

STUDIES ON THE NEW TESTAMENT.

Edited by the Hon. and Rev. W. H. LYTTELTON, M.A., Rector of Hagley, and Hon. Canon of Worcester.

"Unquestionably M. Godet is one of the first, if not the very first, of contemporary commentators on the Scripture. His portraits and his descriptions are projected upon the canvas with a brilliancy of the oxyhydrogen light, 'as, compared with the oil-lamp of ordinary comprehension; and we have no hesitation in advising all students of the Scriptures to procure and to read with careful attention these luminous essays."—*Literary Churchman.*

Crown 8vo.   Price 7s. 6d., cloth.

ORIGIN AND HISTORY OF THE NEW TESTAMENT.

With Appendix on Apocryphal Writings.

By JAMES MARTIN, B.A.,
Translator of "Keil and Delitzsch on the Minor Prophets," "Ebrard's Gospel History," etc., etc.

Third Edition.   Small 8vo, cloth.   Price 3s. 6d.

A YOUNG MAN'S DIFFICULTIES WITH HIS BIBLE.

By the Rev. D. W. FAUNCE, D.D.,
Author of "The Christian in the World."

Contents :—The Young Man's Book—Is the Bible True?—Is the Bible Inspired?—Difficulties as to Miracles—Difficulties from Geology—Difficulties from Astronomy—Difficulties about Historic Facts.

Third Thousand.   Cloth, Fcap. 8vo.   Price 2s. 6d.

PERSONAL VISITS TO THE GRAVES OF EMINENT MEN.

By the Rev. JAMES BARDSLEY, M.A.,
Rector of St. Ann's, Manchester, and Honorary Canon of the Cathedral.

"The book is admirably done, the style is smooth, graphic, and clear, and altogether there are few works so small that contain so much."—*Art Journal.*
"In this volume Mr. Bardsley has given us a series of sketches of representative Churchmen. The result is eminently satisfactory. Every life has its lessons, and these are admirably brought out by Mr. Bardsley."—*Rock.*

Fcap. 8vo, cloth.   Price 3s. 6d.

LONDON: HODDER & STOUGHTON, 27, PATERNOSTER ROW.

www.ingramcontent.com/pod-product-compliance
Lightning Source LLC
Chambersburg PA
CBHW031441160426
43195CB00010BB/806